MENTORING MINDSET, SKILLS AND TOOLS 10TH ANNIVERSARY EDITION

EVERYTHING YOU NEED TO KNOW AND DO TO
MAKE MENTORING WORK

ANN ROLFE

Mentoring Works

Mentoring Mindset, Skills and Tools
10th Anniversary Edition

By
Ann Rolfe

©2022 Mentoring Works
Synergetic People Development Pty Limited
ISBN 978-0-9872765-4-4

CONTENTS

FOREWORD

Welcome to the *Mentoring Mindset, Skills and Tools 10th Anniversary Edition.*

Thank you for buying this book.

It's been 10 years since I started to put the material I taught mentors and mentees in my workshops into this book. I wanted practical, down-to-earth information to be available to everyone in mentoring programs or mentoring informally so that mentoring would be easier, enjoyable and even more effective. In my own programs, I liked that there was one book for both mentors and mentees, where they could literally be on the same page.

In 2020, I released the 4th edition. It was a rocky year for most of us, I began wondering whether mentoring was even relevant anymore. I soon realised that mentoring was, in fact, more important than ever. It presents us with some extra challenges, however. So I delivered a webinar: *Mentoring in the Current Crisis*, which you can view here and put the same content into a free ebook that you can download here.

Now I've retired as a trainer, consultant, and coach after more than 30 years helping organisations set up and run mentoring programs, train mentors and mentees and provide career development. I continue to be devoted to making accessible my life's work in mentoring, career and strengths-based development through books and free webinars. I've written *The Mentor's Toolkit for Career Conversations* and *Advanced Mentoring Skills* and I present regular, free webinars. You can see the details and register here.

Just to let you know, I'm (a UK born) Australian. That means if you are from the USA you're going to notice some different spelling of words than you're used to. For example, we use s instead of z quite often and have u in words like behaviour and colour. I hope that doesn't get in the way of you finding this book useful.

If you'd like to contact me, please do
ann@mentoring-works.com

INTRODUCTION

Is it strange that something as old as mentoring has so much to offer in the contemporary environment?

What began around the campfires in the caves of pre-historic humans was immortalised in ancient Greek myths and institution-alised in 21st century organisations. However, mentoring has evolved, it is dynamic, personal and practical. It is in demand and valued. Organisations see its strategic worth and individuals enjoy many benefits. Mentoring conversations and relationships are embedded in professional, family and social life.

Mentoring comes easily and naturally to a few. Others *think* they're good at it. The rest of us know there's plenty of scope to improve our ability to mentor and be mentored. This book aims to help you make mentoring easy, enjoyable, and effective.

Is This Book for You?

If you are a **mentee**, this book will help you:

- Organise and plan your mentoring
- Focus on goals

- Generate ideas, actions, and outcomes, and
- Reflect on your progress.

If you are a **mentor**, this book provides:

- Proven techniques for leading a mentoring conversation
- Sample questions and conversation starters
- Guidelines and practical tools to make mentoring easier, more enjoyable and effective

I've written this book for both mentors and mentees because both need the right mindset, skills, and tools to make mentoring a productive and satisfying experience.

And, if you are a **manager, team leader or supervisor**, you'll see how you can integrate mentoring into your personal leadership style to improve results.

The Original Mentor

According to ancient Greek mythology, a warrior king, Odysseus, left his island home of Ithaca to fight the Trojan War. He knew he'd be gone for a very long time. In fact, he and his men would be away for over ten years, in a journey that became known as the Odyssey, in Homer's epic poem. They fought the war, got lost on their way home and had terrible adventures.

The story goes that before the King left, he entrusted his son and heir, Prince Telemachus to the care of a wise old friend, to help the boy grow and develop, ready to take his rightful place should his father not return. The name of this trusted guide was Mentor.

But we're talking Greek mythology here, an epic about the king's travels, heroes, monsters, and sorcerers. Mortals were the playthings of the gods. So, in Homer's epic it was not Mentor but the Greek goddess, Athena who guided and protected the young prince. She appeared in many human forms, first as a chieftain named Mentes and later as the king's friend Mentor.

In the original story, Mentor was a minor player charged with keeping the king's household intact. A task at which he failed. So, when did Mentor turn into the "wise guide"?

Mentor's role was revamped in a sequel to Homer's Odyssey, '*Les Aventures de Télémaque*' written in 1699 by French educator, Fenelon who promoted the pedagogical, teacher-pupil relationship originally associated with mentoring. The term protégé, a label often given to the person being mentored, comes from French and means "one who is protected". It is derived from Athena's actions in Homer's Odyssey.

Over time, mentoring morphed into master-apprentice roles in trades and patron-protégés in arts, and teacher-pupil relationships. Sometimes mentors were sponsors who hand-picked successors or favourites and gave them special advantages.

21st century mentoring is different, and it's just as well. Todays' mentees, be they young workers, mature workers, women or minorities, are turned off by a pedagogical approach. It's ineffective in unlocking potential and can be downright detrimental to the retention and engagement of talent.

That's not to say that people don't look to those with experience and those in roles they aspire to for mentorship. What it means is, if we hold on to old ideas about mentoring relationships, we've got it wrong and we are limiting people's development.

Mentoring itself is about evolution - learning, advancement, and personal and professional growth. It is for those who proactively develop themselves. It has a ripple effect because one's development influences others. Mentoring advances all of us to new levels as human beings.

Workplace mentoring has become a two-way, more reciprocal relationship. Almost every mentor I speak with talks about a shift in themselves because of mentoring. They gain personal insight, review their own goals and strategies and learn from the person they interact with. Mentoring is no longer so much about one giving and the other receiving. It is more a partnership where both gain value.

Today, we build mentoring on trust, respect, and mutuality. It may happen organically when you spontaneously develop an informal mentoring relationship. Or, you may select or be matched with a mentoring partner in a more structured mentoring program.

There is a growing role for managers as mentors. Managers have always been responsible for performance, but emerging thinking and practice are changing. Now the trend is to regular feedback conversations led by managers. With employee engagement at just 13% worldwide and managers accountable for 70% of the variance[1], a manager who mentors and coaches his or her team-members is vital.

The next leap forward, I believe is mentorship—where leadership and mentoring merge. I'm speaking of the leadership that each of us takes regardless of job title, age or status, merging with the dynamic mentoring I describe in this book. By our words and actions, we will support and challenge others in conversations that both elicit and impart wisdom.

PART I

MENTORING DEFINED

1

WHY BE OR HAVE A MENTOR?

The world is changing around us at a speed never seen before. Transformation disrupts whole industries. New technologies wipe out jobs, and new ones emerge. A new generation enters the workplace where elders stay on, if they can. There is no status-quo. We worry:

- How do we keep up?
- Will we adapt?
- Can we have fulfilling, ongoing careers?

There is so much information at our fingertips. We are drowning in data, buried by information overload. We can gather knowledge from search engines and know-how from YouTube. Often, we are force-fed opinions and skewered by facts (alternate or otherwise)! It makes you wonder:

- How do we make sense of it all?
- To what practical use can we put it?
- Where do we gain insight?

We are learning more about the brain. Neuroscience reveals stunning complexity. What we once thought of as the seat of logic and rational thinking, we now discover is ruled by emotions. Hair-trigger reactions flying down neural pathways combine with pre-programmed personality to stimulate behavioural responses.

- How do we relate to one-another?
- What does it take to communicate?
- Can we learn to manage ourselves?

One-on-one and in groups, mentoring conversations helps us discover our own answers to these and many more questions and challenges. Mentoring helps us develop personally and professionally and grow as human beings.

Benefit of Mentoring

If you have ever had an excellent mentor, you know the value of having a person who asks questions that make you think, someone who listens without judging you. Who will, if you ask, offer their opinion or ideas but make sure that you make your own decisions about what you want to do. Here's what some mentees said about their experience:

"Amazingly positive. I'm more confident."
"I now believe in myself, trust my own judgment."
"I didn't know I needed a mentor, but now I know it's not just about getting advice, and I see what I've been able to do, I'd recommend it to anyone."

What do Mentors get out of it?

MOST MENTORS HAVE ALTRUISTIC MOTIVATION; they volunteer to mentor for personal satisfaction, the desire to assist others, or the wish to give something back. We should recognise and acknowledge the generosity of people who mentor. However, mentors often tell me they feel they gain as much from mentoring as do the people they mentor. Senior managers said of their experience as mentors:

"The myth that the mentee does all the learning is wrong."
"I was inspired. It was life-changing, a very personal experience, and I gained a new perspective on many things."
"It was a chance to develop a relationship with a person you might never otherwise interact with."

The main aims of workplace mentoring are personal, professional, and career development for the mentee. Yet mentors report that they enhance their communication, become better leaders and develop their own career skills because of mentoring others. Some management development programs require participants to mentor others as part of their own professional growth process.

Both mentor and mentee develop as a result of the conversations you have. Your personal and professional growth builds organisational capability.

Tacit Knowledge

You will tap into tacit knowledge. That means drawing out knowledge, understanding and wisdom underlying the experience that you and your mentoring partner have. For organisations, this is a vital hidden resource.

Many organisations use mentoring for knowledge management, recognising that the implicit knowledge in experienced workers' heads is too valuable not to pass on. For mentors, mentoring is a better way to "know what you know". Sharing knowledge with someone else deepens your understanding and appreciation of your own expertise. Mentees learn why and how certain actions produce outcomes. Questions help you re-examine and perhaps change what you know.

Wellbeing

Much more attention is being paid to well-being at work and people are more aware of the importance of relationships and communication in reducing stress. Neuroscience is identifying ways to create and strengthen neural pathways and stimulate growth in parts of the brain vital to mental health. They have shown that the act of giving (or even observing someone else give, or help another) stimulates areas of the brain that release the feel-good chemical dopamine.

Mentoring does more than make people feel good. It provides a timeout for thinking and reflecting. It encourages creative and critical thinking, goal setting and planning. You learn to be present, to listen consciously, to ask good questions, all attributes that can improve the quality of your life. Connecting, building relationships, and the thought process used in mentoring contribute to your well-being. This can add to organisational productivity.

Perspective

Developing a relationship with someone you might not otherwise meet, someone older or younger, from another part of the organisation or in some other way different from you, expands your perspective. Scientific research is now showing that difference, dissent and discordant ideas make us smarter![1] By listening to someone else, you will gain a new perspective. Seeing more than one point of view increases the intelligence you bring to any situation.

Mentoring builds the confidence to acknowledge differences and respectfully disagree. It reduces resistance and defensiveness and allows you to explore ideas dissimilar to your own. This can produce more harmony, creativity, and productivity.

Activity: What Do You Want From Mentoring?

Tick any that apply to you and add your own ideas to the list.

Mentees

- Discover and develop your talents and skills
- Discuss your career aspirations and options
- Set goals and strategies for achieving them
- Receive feedback on your ideas
- Receive encouragement and support
- Tap into informal communication channels
- Learn the "unwritten rules"
- Gain a new or different perspective
- Identify strengths and explore potential
- Raise your profile within, or outside of, your organisation
- Be challenged, use talents and share expertise
- Network and expand contacts
- Receive support during a transition phase
- Personal effectiveness, prioritising and time management
- Learn new skills and extend knowledge and ability
- Access role models
- Get a more strategic view of the organisation
- Develop a better balance of work and personal life
- Prepare job applications and interview skills
- Complete a course of study
- Access a variety of resources
- Discuss work issues
- Develop your leadership capability
- Enter a new environment

Mentors

This list includes altruistic motivators and other reasons cited by mentors.

- Provide encouragement and support to others
- Help them discover and develop their talents and skills
- Discuss their career aspirations and options

- Give support during a transition phase
- Contribute to the leadership capability of others
- Give a more strategic view of the organisation
- Act as a positive role model
- Help build your organisation or profession
- To give something back
- Be challenged, use your talents and share your expertise
- Gain a new or different perspective
- Get a better understanding of younger people, women, or different cultural groups in your workplace
- Network and expand your contacts
- Develop your own leadership capability
- Learn new skills that extend your knowledge and ability
- Reflect on your own career path
- Learn about a different part of the organisation
- See your workplace from a newcomer's point of view
- Personal satisfaction
- Refresh your thinking and attitudes
- Learn about technology from a digital native
- Supercharge your communication skills
- Take time out for meaningful conversations
- Stimulation, energy, and enthusiasm
- Stretch your mind
- Inspiration

Managers

Here are some reasons managers are adopting a mentoring style:

- Develop staff and increase return on investment in all types of learning activities
- Improve performance and productivity through individual guidance and feedback
- Engagement and retention of talented people

- Building individual and team strengths and developing people's capabilities and competence
- Enable people to take responsibility for themselves and the quality of the work
- Demonstrate trust, respect and dependable leadership

2

MENTORING DEFINED

There's no single definition of mentoring. There are many types of mentoring and even experts have differing views about what mentoring really is. I once attended a conference where an academic reported she had found *five hundred* different definitions of mentoring!

I'll offer you a selection of definitions because it is important that any mentoring program or relationship adopts or devises their own definition. Mentors and mentees must clearly understand what's expected of them.

Traditional mentoring pairs an expert with a novice. It has overtones of a master-apprentice or patron-protégé relationship. However, contemporary mentoring expands older ideas so that participants are more equal partners in mentoring, and both enjoy benefits. Sometimes a mentor is older or in a more senior position and therefore more experienced, but it is the quality of the conversation, the thoughtfulness of the questions, and the deep listening that makes mentoring work.

Mentoring is for you if you want to learn and grow. Whether you choose to be a mentor or mentee, it's about setting and achieving goals, facing challenges, solving problems and developing your knowledge, skills and ability.

The purpose of mentoring is personal and/or professional development. It can allow you to flourish as a human being and improve your work and opportunities. It will help you on a career path, or if you want to find your direction or change course.

A mentoring relationship is unique in that the mentor has no vested interest in outcomes other than positive intention for the mentee. A mentor cares, but does not interfere. They are not your boss - they don't have the authority to tell you what to do. They assist you in making informed decisions about what you want and how to get it.

Definitions

A mentor enables the mentee to move toward their chosen goals with the benefit of their own insight
and (possibly) advice or input based on the mentor's experience.

Two keywords this definition are "enables" - a mentor doesn't do the work for the mentee, and "insight" - a mentor causes the mentee to reflect and draw upon their own inner wisdom. Mentoring conversations often produce an "ah ha" moment of recognition or understanding, a sense of revealed truth that comes from within. Here are more definitions from other sources:

"Mentors are helpers. Their style ranges from that of a persistent encourager who helps us build self-confidence, to that of a stern taskmaster who teaches us to appreciate excellence in performance. Whatever their style, they care about us and what we are trying to do."

Shea, Gordon (1992) <u>Mentoring - A Practical Guide.</u> Crisp Publications

"Mentoring is a natural phenomenon that is occurring every day of our lives and, as a result, it directly or indirectly affects the quality of learning and performance in the workplace."

Rylatt, Alistair (1994) <u>Learning Unlimited.</u> Business and Professional Publishing

"a wise and trusted counselor or teacher."
Dictionary.com"

A developmental process, which may in some forms involve a transfer of skill or knowledge from a more experienced person to a less experienced, through learning, dialogue and role modelling. In other forms may be a partnership for mutual learning between peers or across differences such as age, race or discipline."

European Mentoring and Coaching Council Task Force 2010

Here are more of my own definitions:

An alliance,
that creates a space for dialogue,
that results in reflection, action and learning.

Conversations that create insight.

A synergetic relationship - two or more people, engaged in a process that achieves more than each could alone.

Interaction with another that facilitates personal and professional development.
Strategic planning for individuals

The table below shows how mentoring has changed. It will continue to evolve. You shape your mentoring relationship to make it work for you. The activities in this chapter let you pause, consider and discuss with your mentoring partner, just how the two of you will apply these ideas.

Traditional Paradigm	Contemporary Thinking
The mentor picks a protégé	You look for mentors
A mentor is someone more senior	A mentor is someone you can learn from regardless of age or position
You should have a lot in common with your mentor	Difference provides potential for greater discovery, challenge and growth
Mentoring is for young people	Mentoring can be helpful at any stage
You have one mentor	You may have mentors for different aspects of life and career
Mentoring is one-to-one	Mentoring may be individual or in a group
Mentors tell you what to do	Mentor is a sounding board
Mentors give advice	Mentors assist your decision-making and problem-solving

Traditional Paradigm/Contemporary Thinking

There is no "one-size fits all". We can tailor mentoring to suit individuals, circumstances, and the outcomes you want. There are many ways to mentor, such as one-to-one, group, reverse and my favourite, reciprocal mentoring.

Informal Mentoring

Mentoring conversations happen by chance with people you meet or people you know. The person may give you useful information, share their experience or just listen while you think out loud. It may be a one-off conversation or a lifelong relationship. The word "mentor" may never be used.

People fondly think this type of organic mentoring is best and that may be so - if you are lucky enough to stumble upon the right person at the right rime. However, I've spoken to enough people who have had bad mentoring experiences to know that it doesn't always work out.

Often, those who could most benefit from mentoring miss out if we leave mentoring to chance.

It's still true that most mentoring takes place informally, but people can mean very different things by "mentoring". If you intend to be mentored informally, ask for what you want and use the ideas in this book to get what you need. If you are a mentor, facilitate a discussion that establishes the purpose and the parameters of the relationship. This book will show you how.

Formal Mentoring

Formal mentoring relationships are usually part of a structured program. You may be matched, introduced, and supported in developing the mentoring partnership. Roles and responsibilities will be clearly defined. There will be a discussion of expectations, goals, and the process to be used. The frequency and duration of contact is agreed and ground-rules are established. Progress will be monitored and there will be help if the relationship doesn't work out so that you can make a no-fault exit.

Reverse-mentoring

In the old paradigm, mentoring means a more senior person (in terms of age, position or experience) mentors a junior. Reverse mentoring places the more junior person as the mentor. We use reverse mentoring when executives need to understand operations or technology that shop-floor, front-line or tech-savvy employees can share. Young people who have grown up with social media for example, can convey the value and benefits and the practical ways to use it. In such a rapidly changing world, senior people can't afford to be left behind!

Reverse-mentoring can bridge the generation gap when a relationship of trust and understanding is built. The key to success in reverse mentoring is the ability to create and maintain an attitude of openness to the experience and dissolve the barriers of status, power and position.

Reciprocal Mentoring

Two people form a mentoring partnership and take turns in mentoring each other as peers. This is very much a two-way street with each able to ask the other for input and advice and each providing a listening ear in a confidential conversation. Each one facilitates the mentoring process by asking questions, listening and reflecting. As in most types of mentoring, there is a place for offering another perspective, expressing an opinion or providing information. However, the decision-making responsibility always resides with the person who will implement action and experience the consequences. Because the partners recognise each other as peers, it can be easier to offer and receive input as information rather than advice.

Group Mentoring

Group mentoring involves one mentor meeting with several mentees at the same time. For example, new graduates in their first workplace, women with common goals, or entrepreneurs. A wonderful synergy can develop in this environment. As the mentor poses questions, listens and reflects he or she draws all members of the group into the conversation. Each one has their own experience and insight to share and can take their own learning from the discussion.

In a **mastermind** a group of peers interact in a conversation or think-tank. The original concept was described by Napolean Hill as:

"... a group of brains, co-ordinated (or connected) in a spirit of harmony, will provide more thought energy than a single brain, just as a group of electric batteries will provide more energy than a single battery ... the increased energy created by that alliance becomes available to every brain in the group."

Mentoring circles are a variation of group mentoring that led by one or more mentors that may blend elements of peer mentoring and mastermind groups.

Mentoring Moments

Mentoring moments are those times you take the opportunity to have a conversation that creates insight, explores options or provides guidance, while you are doing something else. They happen in the workplace, at home, during leisure activities and are simply an extension of normal conversation.

eMentoring/Virtual Mentoring

People used to talk about ementoring as if it were a different form of mentoring, but today we are so used to conducting conversations online that the term is more or less redundant. It is not unusual for mentoring partners never to meet face-to-face, yet have effective and productive relationships. There are many ways for online mentoring to occur, from dedicated and secure purpose-built platforms to video conferencing, FaceTime calls, messaging apps and email. It may take more effort to develop rapport, but it can be easier and more convenient than face-to-face, and some people will actually prefer the online option.

Mentoring or Coaching?

If you're a mentee you may want to think about whether you need a mentor or a coach. If you are a mentor, you'll need to consider the type of assistance you are able to give.

Most people agree there are differences between the two, and have various ideas about what mentoring and coaching are. What one calls mentoring, another may call coaching. Regardless of what you call the process, unrealistic or dissimilar expectations can undermine its effectiveness.

There are also many different types of mentoring and coaching. My focus is on workplace mentoring which is most often associated with career development. I contrast it with performance coaching in the workplace that that focuses on a person's ability to do their job. I use the following distinctions:

Performance Coach: a person who trains, tutors or prepares an individual for improved skill and performance.

Mentor: one who guides and stimulates an individual's reflection and actions for improved personal and professional outcomes.

The table below shows the distinctions between these types of mentoring and coaching.

Performance Coaching	Mentoring
Supports achievement of specific goals	Enables self-development of broad capabilities
Action oriented	Reflection emphasis
Concentrates on small steps	Concerned with bigger picture
Attends to gap between actual and desired performance	Facilitates personal goal setting, planning and action
Features practice of required performance, feedback and correction	Based on conversation, problem-solving, decision-making, creative and critical thinking processes
Results can be measured objectively	Results may be subjective and difficult to measure
Behavioural outcomes evident within prescribed timeframe	Insight, personal and professional growth evolves over an indefinite time

Performance Coaching/Mentoring

These types of mentoring and coaching both:

- Provide one-to-one interaction to achieve personalised learning and growth

- Cater to individual needs, personal styles and time constraints
- Can be conducted face to face or from remote locations
- Complement formal training and educational experiences
- Process real-life issues, problems and decisions
- Facilitate access to information and choices about new behaviours and actions
- Support the achievement of positive outcomes.

Performance coaching is used when there is a well-defined goal that is based on improving skills and the ability to do specific tasks in the current job. It is a role for managers and supervisors who are responsible for developing their subordinates or specialists who have technical expertise.

Mentoring is appropriate for career planning, providing general guidance, setting and achieving personal goals, making decisions or facilitating problem solving. It is usually "off-line" that is, the mentor has no authority over the mentee.

Activity:

Discuss with your mentoring partner the scope of the development you have in mind and the style of relationship you want.

3

MENTORING ROLES AND RESPONSIBILITIES

Mentoring is a method of goal setting and planning. The mentor's role is to facilitate a conversation that enables the mentee to choose and implement a course of action. A mentor may provide information, share their experience, or express an opinion. However, it is always the mentee that decides, acts, and produces outcomes.

The Mentoring Dynamic

Mentoring relationships are rich and complex. They are flexible and dynamic. The mentoring purpose is to both support and challenge the mentee. The process involves eliciting and imparting information.

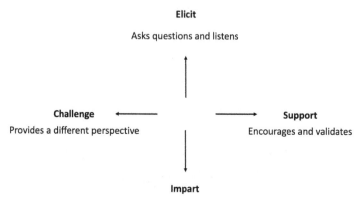

The Mentoring Dynamic

Mentors must first build rapport so they can elicit information from the mentee. Mentors ask questions, listen, then ask more questions. They listen to ensure that they understand the goals and needs of the mentee before they ever impart information. Mentors share their knowledge, experience, ideas and opinions when invited and when it is appropriate to do so.

Often people need support from the mentor, validation or affirmation, but sometimes it is a challenge that brings out our best. So, a mentor is an empathetic ally who, occasionally, can challenge the mentee by disagreeing, giving a different point of view, or suggesting a different course of action. A mentor imparts information. However, it is up to the mentee to decide what to do because they have to live with the consequences of their actions.

Mentoring Roles

Mentoring conversations are confidential, so the mentor becomes a confidante, someone trusted enough to share dreams, aspirations and issues with. Sometimes, all people need is quiet listening. Simply speaking their thoughts out loud generates insight and solutions or actions, then becomes obvious to them. So the mentor, just by being supportive, is a catalyst for change. A mentor is often a sounding board so that the mentee can "bounce ideas off them". Mentors often link their mentee to other resources or people that can provide information. The mentor doesn't have to have all the answers! The mentor is a role model, their behaviour and approach provide an example. Coaching may be a subset of mentoring. If asked, a mentor may help the mentee develop specific skills and abilities. People who want mentoring sometimes want an adviser. They value the knowledge, ideas, and opinions that come from experience. The mentor elicits the mentee's own thoughts before offering advice as additional options. A mentor is also a guide. A mentor has a "duty of care". If the mentee intends action that could have seriously adverse results, the mentor helps the mentee become more aware of those consequences. If they cannot prompt insight, the mentor can share their own concerns with the mentee.

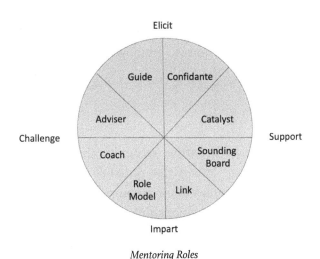

Mentoring Roles

The mentor's job is to listen, provide constructive feedback, help the mentee consider various options, refer them to resources available and facilitate their decision-making regarding work or career matters. The mentor may share his or her own experiences and, if asked, give advice. Mentors provide guidance without being directive.

The mentor does not solve the mentee's problems; rather they are a collaborator in a problem-solving process.

Confusion regarding the role and responsibilities can lead to disappointment and dissatisfaction so it is important to discuss them at the beginning.

Confidentiality

Mentors and mentees should agree to keep the content of their conversations confidential. The responsibility lies with both parties to respect the trust of the other. However, use good judgement. If you do not feel safe or it's not appropriate to reveal certain information, don't. You must not share privileged information.

A mentor is not a doctor, lawyer or priest, and certain activities are outside the agreed confidentiality between a mentor and mentee. Review written policies or talk to the mentoring program coordinator to clarify your responsibilities. In Australia, we are required by law to report incidents of harassment or other unlawful behaviour. Most organisational policy requires employees to report unethical behaviour.

Boundaries

It is important that both parties recognise the limitations of the mentoring relationship. When not qualified to offer advice, the mentor must refer the mentee to other sources. Personal matters such as marriage or sexual relationships, violence, drugs, alcohol, gambling, ill health and grief are examples of personal issues that you should refer to experienced specialist counsellors. Work grievances should be handled through the designated channels. Refer legal, financial, human resources, or other specialist questions to qualified professionals. The program coordinator will advise of resources to deal with these matters.

Phases in a Mentoring Relationship

Some mentoring relationships are open-ended, but most have a finite timeframe and evolve through phases.

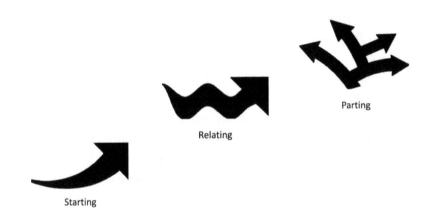

Parting

Relating

Starting

Phases in a Mentoring Relationship

1. Starting

The aim of an initial contact is to see if the mentor and mentee are willing to try to work together.

Some questions the mentor asks himself or herself are:

- Can I make time for mentoring?
- Are there reasons I should?
- Is this person someone I want to assist?

The mentee will want to know, is this person someone I can:

- Learn from?
- Communicate with in confidence?
- Respect and be respected by?

You need to build rapport to talk about the scope of mentoring. What is it that the mentee is seeking? What can the mentor offer? This might be enough in an initial contact. Often, you'll want time to think about whether to proceed to the next step.

A follow-up conversation will include discussion of roles and expectations. Use the activities in this chapter and the Tools and Guides section to help you. Getting clear will allow each of you to make an informed decision about starting a mentoring relationship together.

The first one or two meetings will also involve planning practical aspects (like when, where, and how to get together). You may use a written agreement, such as the one provided in the Tools and Guides, to summarise your commitment. It is also important to talk about the purpose and expected benefits of mentoring. You may be able to set some goals at this stage or you may want more time and discussion to allow them to emerge.

At your third meeting, do a quick review and check that you both want to commit to an ongoing relationship. If you have doubts or want to exit and you're in a formal program, the coordinator will help you sort out difficulties or exit the relationship. Not everyone "clicks" and sometimes mismatches happen, so it's better to end it and move on.

2. Growing

Once there is an agreement to start a mentoring, you concentrate on getting to know one another and developing the relationship. How much you share depends on you and your mentoring partner. For some, mentoring is quite relaxed and friendly. It is professionally oriented and relevant to the agreed purpose of mentoring, but includes social elements like meeting for coffee or lunch. Others prefer a business-like approach and more formal meetings.

In the growth phase, expect to share ideas, give and receive feedback. You may focus your mentoring on one specific goal with a subset of strategies planned to achieve it over time. Or it might be a series of discussions about current issues, options or decisions.

The mentor:

- Takes the lead, setting the tone and facilitating the conversation
- Makes sure that the purpose of the mentoring is kept in mind
- Manages time effectively during the meeting

The mentee:

- Comes to meetings prepared with issues for discussion or questions to explore, perhaps sending the mentor a list of bullet points that set the agenda
- Describes actions and progress since their last conversation
- Shares insights and lessons learned by reflecting on their experiences

Things may change as the mentor and mentee interact. You should regularly review the mentoring relationship and the process you are using. Talk about what works well and what you'd prefer to do differently. *Structure the Meeting* in the Tools and Guides section of this book provides an outline, including a debrief that helps you keep on track over the life of your mentoring.

4. Parting

Once the mentoring goals have been achieved or the specified period of ends, it's time to evaluate the process and the outcomes. There are some questions to help you with this in *Evaluate Your Mentoring Relationship* in the Mentoring Tools and Guides section of this book.

The mentor:

- Reviews the original goals of mentoring and the actual outcomes
- Reflects on the process they used and its effectiveness
- Provides feedback to program organisers and/or their mentee

The mentee:

- Takes stock of what they have achieved and how they utilised the opportunity
- Acknowledges the contribution of the mentor
- Provides feedback to program organisers and/or their mentor

If you are in a mentoring program, there may be formal closure, marked with an event or celebration. Sometimes friendship or reciprocal mentoring has evolved and mentoring partners continue meeting informally. Others are happy simply to conclude the relationship. Not every mentoring relationship is an unqualified success, but each one offers you something to learn from.

Activity:

In the "Mentoring Tools and Guides" section of this book, take a look at:

1. A Guide to Roles and Responsibilities
2. The Mentoring Code
3. The Mentoring Agreement Template
4. A Mentoring Plan
5. Structure the Meeting
6. Pre/Post Meeting Checklist
7. A Guide to Roles and Responsibilities

8. The Mentoring Code
9. Activity: Expectations
10. The Mentoring Agreement

Discuss the roles and responsibilities listed with your mentoring partner, decide which you will each adopt.

4

MENTORING AND LEARNING

Instruction, coaching, and mentoring are strategies to help us learn. I see each of them on a continuum, with training at one end and development at the other (see the diagram below). That said, there can be overlap between the roles of instructor, coach, and mentor.

Instruction, on the job, in a classroom or online, involves someone *teaching skills required for a specific task*. This means analysing a task and identifying the knowledge or behaviours required to perform it. The instructor then shows and/or tells the person how it's done and supervises their practice. The instructor monitors and tests the learner until they achieve a satisfactory standard of performance.

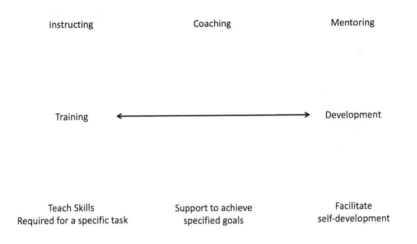

The Learning Continuum

Coaching (in this context) provides *support to achieve specified goals*. It is like sports coaching, where an expert on the sidelines observes a person perform. The coach has the expertise to identify what the person needs to do better. A tennis coach may say: "you need to work on your serve" and will provide guidance, whether it is technique, building strength or stamina or perhaps psychological exercise to achieve the desired result. The coach gives feedback and corrects form. Their focus is current performance. On-the-job coaching is essential to ensure transfer of learning after training courses. In fact, in most cases, only about 16% of learning is applied when there is no on-the-job coaching![1]

In instruction and this type of coaching, someone other than the individual has usually determined the performance goals and methods of learning.

Mentoring aims to facilitate self-development. Goals may be specific or broad, general, even quite fuzzy. It's not unusual for people to enter mentoring with quite vague outcomes in mind. They feel it will be good for them, but are not really sure what they expect to gain. The mentor may need to help the mentee figure out what they want and why it's important. It's fine to work toward general aims such as career or professional development in the beginning. Later, the mentee will set more specific goals and you'll determine joint goals for the relationship.

Instruction, coaching and mentoring are not mutually exclusive. Many excellent instructors and teachers also coach and mentor. Coaching can move from one end of the learning continuum to the other. A mentor can move into coaching or instructing. However, the mentor only does so where they have the relevant expertise and at the invitation of the mentee.

Instruction, coaching and mentoring all provide support for an individual's development. However, instruction and coaching are concerned with immediate performance and specific skills. Mentoring is focussed on moving toward the future, by building capability and facilitating personal growth.

Learning in the Workplace

Learning in the workplace means more than training courses. In fact, Research from The Centre for Creative Leadership (CCL) has found that only 10% of the learning leaders use at work come from formal education and training[2]. 20% is learned from other people, but most learning is a result of on-the-job experience - making mistakes and dealing with challenges.

The formula 70:20:10, first used by Bob Eichinger and Mike Lombardo is based on original research by CCL has been adopted by many organisations to guide a blended learning approach.

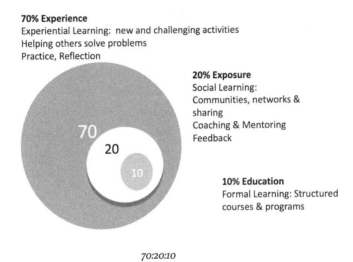

70% Experience
Experiential Learning: new and challenging activities
Helping others solve problems
Practice, Reflection

20% Exposure
Social Learning:
Communities, networks &
sharing
Coaching & Mentoring
Feedback

10% Education
Formal Learning: Structured
courses & programs

70:20:10

10 **Education** includes formal education and training that usually takes place off-the-job, such as conferences, courses, workshops, seminars, usually face-to-face—all the stuff I love to do both as presenter and participant! And if you're like me, maybe you're wondering why this type of learning only makes up 10% of what we use at work. After all, we spend years at school, college or university and attend numerous formal training courses. We've seen an increase in e-learning. Some of it is great, with engaging simulations or gamification, but some online learning is not much more than an electronic book with multiple-choice questions to check we've read it. This kind of learning is important, but it is not always transferred or applied in the workplace.

20 **Exposure** is where role models, mentoring or coaching are most evident - showing, telling, giving feedback to reinforce or correct performance. It also includes peer learning, communities of practice, master-mind groups, team collaboration, personal learning networks and learning circles.

70 **Experience** could be called "learning by doing". We learn how to do routine tasks and, with practice, become more competent. Our experience may make us more confident, capable and quicker. More than that, we may figure out more efficient ways to get the job done.

We build systems of continuous improvement on the understanding that worker's experience allows them to see possibilities for efficiencies and greater effectiveness. Japan is a leader in this field. One reason the quality of cars has gone up while costs have come down is worker input to improve production lines.

70:20:10 isn't an either/or choice. All three are important and add value. They work best when you take an integrated approach to learning, and better still, when you include mentoring in all aspects of learning.

How Mentors Improve Learning

1. Mentors boost the return on investment of off-the-job learning.
2. Mentors can ensure that self-directed learning is acknowledged and put to good use.
3. Mentors encourage the reflection needed to learn from experience.

Education - formalised learning: Although it represents the smallest part of the 70:20:10 formula, education and training are the most expensive part of workplace learning. The cost of taking people away from the workplace, travel and accommodation as well as course or conference fees mean that it really must provide a good return on investment to be worth it. Increasingly, leaner budgets allow less off-sites. They are a luxury, but they can be effective.

Post pandemic, more, if not most, training and education will be delivered remotely rather than face-to-face. The benefits and pitfalls remain, in that very little learning is applied in the workplace in any meaningful way, without coaching or mentoring.

Of course, *managers* should discuss the purpose of any training or education before the learner starts. The manager and employee should talk about why the learning is needed, what the objectives and expected benefits are, and how it applies to the employee's work now and in the future. The manager should flag that there will be a follow-up conversation.

After the event, they should talk about outcomes, actions, support, and plans for ongoing feedback. If the manager-employee conversation doesn't happen, mentoring before and after the event is essential to gain full value from the learning.

Best Practice for the "10" Education (Off-the-job learning):

- Provides engaging pre and post learning activities
- Requires managers to plan with employees before and after any off-the-job learning event
- Compliments all training and education with mentoring or coaching
- Empowers employees to manage their own development
- Supports proactive learners

Exposure – social learning: People learn from the norms presented to them by colleagues in the workplace, so exposure to the right role models is vital. They absorb attitudes, values and behaviours from the environment. Employees need leaders they can emulate, who show interest and take time to develop them. Investing in on-boarding for new hires is critical.

Today, proactive learners seek feedback, people with whom to debrief, or bounce ideas off. They will reach outside the workplace, using online networks and people in close proximity. These employees are likely to be the organisation's best talent. Mentors can engage them and make it more likely they'll stay.

We are talking about people who are likely to be confident, hungry for development opportunities and mobile. Conversations with a mentor or a leader with mentoring skills are critical to keeping them.

Best Practice for the "20" Exposure

- Commits to mentoring for learning
- Mentors new hires, graduate recruits and interns
- Develops mentoring and coaching skills
- Models "Everyone, Always, Learning"
- Shows proactive learners how to get the most from personal learning networks and mentors

Experiential Learning: Most workplace learning comes from experience - doing day-to-day tasks, taking on a new challenge or project, but we only learn from experience when activate the learning cycle. We have an experience. We pause to reflect, decide to do something different, and act on that decision.

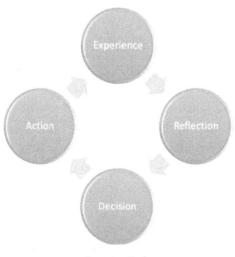

Learning Cycle

I often ask my face-to-face groups: Have you ever made a mistake? Of course most hands go up but a guy once said: "I thought I did once, but I was wrong!" Someone else said: "There's no such thing as a mistake, only a learning experience". But you and I know people who don't learn from their mistakes—they don't even realise they've made one - and you can't learn from experience unless you pause and reflect. Even that won't make a difference unless you make an informed decision - choose to take action.

There's evidence that we learn even more when we reflect on our successes. I once worked with a highly successful project team. They were known for bringing construction projects in on time and within budget. The team manager told me that their secret was the debrief meeting after project completion. The entire team would assemble in a room equipped with whiteboards or flip charts to review the project, discussing what went well, so they could replicate it in future, and what did not go well, so they could avoid that. It was a process of continual learning. The meetings worked because there was no praise or blame involved, simply acceptance of the experience and learning. You can take the shame out of failure, mistakes, or poor performance without reducing accountability by using reflection for learning.

Leadership is critical to experiential learning. Leaders must build relationships and *invite* the learner to reflect on their experience. If there's no reflection, there's no lesson. With reflection, people gain insight from their experience and can use it to improve performance. So whether it's positive reinforcement of what they did well, corrective guidance, or simply noticing whether they are learning the right things - or learning at all—a mentoring conversation adds value. Thinking and reflection can cause insight—awareness, understanding an ah ha moment or epiphany—and a mentor can encourage people to act on what they learn.

Best Practice for the "70" Experience:

- Starts conversations to review events, challenges and problems
- Is curious, collaborative, concerned—asks questions that cause people to reflect
- Facilitates insight—looks for the "ah ha" moment
- Gains commitment to apply learning and offers support
- Follows up and provides positive or corrective feedback

To summarise, mentors, or managers who have mentoring and coaching conversations, add value to all three aspects of the 70:20:10 model. Leading learning in the workplace means that you:

- Activate learning from experience by causing people to reflect on past experience and decide what to do in future. You help them get the right learning from exposure.
- Lead by example. You are a role model; you share tips and tricks, practical guidance and you encourage their use of other mentors, peer learning and other networks.
- Leverage off-the-job learning by discussing what you expect people to gain and why that's important before the training; and how it will be used and supported back on the job after the event.

Activity: What do you want to learn through mentoring?

Discuss what it is each of you plan to learn through mentoring. Think about how the 70:20:10 might be used to gain this learning.

PART II

THE MENTORING PROCESS

5

A MENTORING CONVERSATION

Mentoring conversations facilitate reflection. Conversation can provide the time and conditions conducive to insight. A relationship of rapport and trust heightens the learning available to people when they talk through their experience.

Mentoring conversations need to be confidential and can be free-ranging, taking a holistic approach to the person, their life and work. Mentoring conversations are not just talk. The purpose of creating insight is to capture it and use it to make informed decisions and act on them.

The role of the mentor is to allow a person to talk about their issues and aspirations. They need to draw out the mentee's thoughts and feelings, find out what's important to them and why. Once they understand where the mentee is at, what their current reality is, the mentor may be able to offer useful information. If it's appropriate and relevant, they may share their own experience. So it's important that the mentor knows how and when to elicit and when to impart information. Think of it as a sliding scale, adjusted to the person and the situation.

Sometimes the mentee simply needs support, encouragement, a plan, or practical techniques for getting the outcomes they want. Sometimes they need to be challenged, perhaps even confronted, to bring out their best. Again, different situations call for different strategies.

Such conversations need to be future-focussed. They are strategic and practical, addressing where a person is, where they want to be and how they can get there. An ongoing mentoring relationship helps a person stay on track and fine-tune actions to achieve their outcomes, or re-evaluate and re-set goals.

The model below shows how mentors can lead a reflective conversation that results in constructive action. We want to start talking about the current reality – what's going on for the mentee, the situation or problem and through reflection assist them to make an informed decisions about the action they will take, what they could stop doing or do differently to get a better outcome. So a mentor, firstly initiates exploration of what's going on. The aim is to elicit thoughts and feelings, discover the mentee's values and motivation. Why are they concerned? What's most important to them?

The Mentoring Model

Next, the mentor leads the conversation toward informed decisions. That means they need information. The mentor facilitates the mentee's learning. The mentee may gain information from insight gained through the reflective conversation. Or it may require additional fact-finding—research by the mentee—or perhaps some input from the mentor sharing their own experience.

Once the mentee makes decisions, you can help shape them into goals. The mentor prompts the mentee to describe outcomes, and guides their planning to achieve them, sorting out the actions most likely to get the desired results.

Subsequent conversations support the implementation, following-up, and reviewing actions. Perhaps coaching and reinforcing new behaviours or adjusting the plan.

The Mentoring Conversation

At the heart of the mentoring conversation are four questions. As a mentor, these are not the questions you ask, but the questions you hold in your mind to frame appropriate questions for your particular conversation.

· · ·

QUESTION 1: **Where are you now?**

You want the mentee to reflect on what's going on, clearly understand the current reality, problem, situation, or event, so that they can contribute to the solution. You then want to lead a discussion about what needs to change and why.

QUESTION 2: **Where do you want to be?**

You are comparing and contrasting the current situation and the ideal one. You will provide information and draw on their knowledge so that they make informed decisions and set realistic goals.

QUESTION 3: **How do you get there?**

Having established where they are now and where they want to be, you want your mentee to plan actions to produce outcomes.

QUESTION 4: **How are you doing now?**

Some time later, in a follow-up conversation, you'll lead a review of the action and outcomes and the question that frames that conversation.

There are some sample questions in each of the 4 stages in *Sample Questions*, in the Tools and Guides section of this book. Use them to create your own questions in your own words for your own situation.

The other thing to remember about this model is, while it is a cycle and I've illustrated it as moving in a clockwise fashion from 12 o'clock, you could open your conversation from 2 "Where do you want to be" and then take stock with "where are you now". You may move around in any way that makes sense in the context of your conversation.

Activity: Apply the Framework

For mentors: think of some ways you could comfortably phrase the "Where are you now" question.

For mentees: think about how you'd describe "Where are you now"

6

BE SLOW TO OFFER ADVICE

Mentors don't have all the answers. Nor should they, because it can be far more effective to help mentees find their own insights and choose a course of action for themselves.

Whether someone is telling you about their goal or talking about a challenge, it can be very hard to resist giving advice. You want to help. They've come to you, so they must think you have something to offer. Your instinct is to give an answer. Don't!

People almost always need to *be heard* rather than told what to do.

You've likely experienced how good it feels to just "get something off your chest" with a good listener who is attentive, interested and quiet, simply letting you talk. And, you've probably had an annoying situation when a person couldn't let you simply vent, but had to jump in with "why don't you..." or "you should..."

Autonomy is a basic human need. Individuals want to be in control of their own life and make their own decisions. We don't like feeling weak or ineffectual and even good advice makes us feel inferior because someone else thinks they know better than us.

We feel far better about discussing an issue and being guided to find our own path.

Changing behaviour is hard, but when we have explored an issue in the context of our needs and values and chosen a course based on our own insight, we are more committed to action and likely to follow through.

Here's what to do instead of immediately giving advice.

- Ask questions—"tell me more".
- Make sure you are getting to the real issues—remember, the presenting problem is often not the underlying issue.
- Find out about their needs, wants and values—what's important to them.
- Draw out their ideas. Quite often they will have a strategy and your task is simply to assist them as they make it actionable steps—"so what would you want to do first?"

Only then, if they cannot generate an approach that will work for them, would you offer advice.

- Ask if they want your suggestions, opinion or input.
- Offer it as a possibility, one alternative or something to explore.
- Invite their further thoughts in a way that opens up choices—they decide what to do, and that might be some more thinking or research.

Great mentors don't withhold knowledge or experience, but they are slow to give advice because:

- Old paths and paradigms may be obsolete
- Telling people what to do weakens relationships
- Giving answers stops people thinking for themselves

Old Paths and Paradigms

The world has changed amazingly in the last few decades. Mobile phones have been with us about fifty years and epitomise the revolution in technology. Once, every family home had one TV and one telephone anchored to the wall and teenagers fought over their use. Now everyone in the household has one or more personal devices that screen entertainment, make audio and video calls and do so much more. You can educate and amuse yourself about ancient technology by watching 17-year-olds take on a rotary phone on YouTube[1].

The robots may not be coming for your job, but University of Sydney professor of data science and machine learning, Hugh Durrant-Whyte says "All jobs that are primarily analysis are capable of automation,"[2]. Some of the disappearing jobs may surprise you. They include doctors, lawyers and public servants. It's not all bad news though, because of course, there will be new jobs, just not as we know them.

There have been equally dramatic changes in society, business and the economy. As Marshal Goldsmith points out: "What got you here won't get you there"[3]. Buzz words like career "agility", "resilience" and "reinvention" are common and appropriate.

Expectations of job satisfaction, work-life integration, professional development and progress at work have changed. There is a lot more job mobility, competition for positions, contract work and outsourcing. Career paths are seldom linear, often unpredictable, and change is inevitable, so the past is not a reliable guide to the future.

We will *all* need to learn and adapt our knowledge and skills to changing requirements and advice is quickly obsolete.

Telling People What to do Weakens Relationships

Ever wondered why someone rejects your well-intended, wise advice? Even though you know a clear and beneficial way forward, the other person refuses or cannot see it? Have you offered guidance only for them to become defensive or even aggressive?

The truth is, being told what to do creates an immediate imbalance in a relationship. It implies the status of the advice-giver is higher than the other person. Neuroscience has shown that the brain perceives this as a social threat. The brain reacts exactly as it would to a physical threat by triggering the fight/flight/freeze response. So when you give advice, especially unsolicited input, the automatic response is resistance.

Even when people ask for advice, immediate suggestions, opinions or directions can go awry because you may:

- Not have all the information or be making assumptions
- Be dealing with a superficial issue or symptom, not the real problem
- Judge the situation from your own point-of-view, needs and values

Of course, a mentor can offer information, opinion, suggestions and ideas. However, they must first listen, ask questions, and aim to empower mentees by helping them gain insight.

Giving Answers Stops People Thinking for Themselves

One reason brainstorming—where you generate as many possibilities as you can before stopping to critique them - is so useful, is because the second, or twenty-second, answer may be better than the first. An answer is not necessarily the answer, and your answer may not be my answer. But if people think they have the correct answer, they often cease exploring the issue and can overlook better options.

Insight

They say Archimedes yelled "Eureka!" as he leapt from his bath and ran naked in the street. The word means "I have found it", and has become associated with the excitement and satisfaction of a solution or great idea that suddenly jumps into consciousness.

History is replete with anecdotes of inventions and scientific breakthroughs linked to sudden insight. Most people have experienced an "Aha" moment of brilliant perception, as if a light is switched on. This kind of understanding or knowing is powerful.

Unexpected flashes of insight often occur when the brain is at rest or occupied in pleasant, undemanding tasks, such as sleeping, bathing, walking or driving. The conscious mind, idling like a car in neutral, suddenly shifts into gear and gets traction on an issue that's been floating in the unconscious.

Learning and development professionals know that insight can also be orchestrated through activities in the class-room, experiential learning or action learning, but they know it is the reflection *after* the event that creates insight. Without a well facilitated debrief, you leave learning to chance.

Likewise, life events, work challenges and mistakes are a rich source of personal and professional growth, but without reflective thinking, they may not become learning experiences. Reflection can produce the insight that turns hindsight into foresight. In other words, you don't have to make the same mistake again!

Reflecting on positive outcomes and how they were achieved is just as powerful. But if we don't take time to stop and reflect, learning may not surface. In our overcrowded thinking space, great ideas, innovative solutions, even epiphanies often get lost, and the insight gained is not very useful if you do not apply it.

Reflection

In every day life and at work, a lot of us seem to be sleep-walking away from our greatest asset as human beings. Our ability to think—critically, creatively and reflectively. A bias for *doing* rather than *thinking* robs us of more than opportunities to learn and develop. Lack of reflection stifles critical thinking, elevates a quick-fix mentality, and shuts down exploration of alternatives and possibilities in problem-solving.

Most of us feel better doing something rather than doing nothing.

However, a study[4] found that professional goalies who stayed in centre of the goal *instead* of lunging left or right saved the goal 33% of the time, yet only stayed there 6% of the time. Acting too quickly robbed them of the result. Rushing to action robs us of results too, but some of us don't regard thinking as working. We have to change that. When mentors lead reflective conversations, they teach people to *slow down* to get better results by overcoming the action bias.

Looking back to draw out the lesson makes experience more useful. Reflection can give us more confidence in our ability to achieve our goals, improved work performance, increased resilience. A study[5] of commuters found that people who used travel time to think and plan their work were happier, more productive and less burned out.

There are three major ways people reflect:

1. **Writing**—a reflective journal, learning log, or essay-type responses to questions
2. **Thinking**—musing and pondering, or analysing and critiquing experience in ways that increase self-awareness
3. **Talking**—conversation, responding to thoughtful questions in order to gain insight, discussing alternative courses of action.

Conversations that most empower mentees are the ones that cause them to reflect, generate insight, use critical and creative thinking to develop possible courses of actions to produce the outcomes they want. Sometimes all the mentor needs to do is lead the conversation. Mentors' input and advice can definitely add value, but is best used late in the conversation, not early.

Activity:
Find Sample Questions to stimulate reflection in the "Tools and Guides" section of this book.

7

DISCOVERING VALUES

Your values are an integral part of who you are. They motivate your aspirations, cause your lifestyle preferences, trigger behaviour and reflect your view of the world. In fact, your values, according to Astrid Berg[1], "reveal the meaning and essence of your life as a whole".

Greater self-awareness of values enables you to:

- Make choices that are right for you
- Be more effective in time management
- Be authentic and increase your personal integrity and credibility with others

Values might include concepts such as freedom, forgiveness, respect, wisdom, independence, creativity, spirituality, beauty, family, hard work, luxury, altruism, service to others, fairness, or world peace.

Values are personal beliefs about what is right or wrong, good or bad, worthwhile or not worthwhile. Values allow you to judge what is important. Some are superficial and changeable, like fashion. Others are deeply held and not easily moved, and others change over time and through life experience. We mostly accumulate values from society and our environment, but some are because of our innate personality.

Each of us has a hierarchy of personal values that guide our behaviour. Some values are stronger than others. It is unlikely that two people will have exactly the same set of values in the same order of importance.

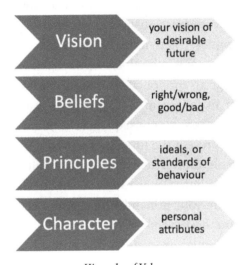

Hierarchy of Values

While you have a hierarchy or priority order of values, this is not static, it is a dynamic and interactive system. Values fade into the background if you do not have clarity about them or don't pay attention to them, or when you are distracted. They can buckle under pressure and can be compromised or subordinated when human needs take precedence in our busy, overstimulating world. Your values are literally at the heart of your relationship with yourself, other people, and the world in general.

This is why mentoring conversations are so important. A mentor's questions can help a mentee think about what is really important to them, raise awareness of what they believe, and identify the values they want to guide their life and career. Discovering values is one of the greatest gifts of mentoring because values influence:

- Every choice you make
- The amount of conflict and stress in your life
- Your priorities - how you manage your time and your life

Values and Choice

You are making choices almost every waking moment of your day. This morning, you decided to get up out of bed. You made that decision consciously or unconsciously. You either thought something to yourself that prompted you to move or you reacted automatically (i.e. without thinking) to some stimulus, like daylight, an alarm clock or even the need to go to the toilet! Your values influence all of these choices. You can make a conscious decision that over-rides your personal values but there are consequences of doing so.

Some values represent the ultimate way you'd like life to be, your vision of a desirable future. You have a set of values or beliefs that contribute to your vision. Other values reflect ideals or standards of behaviour. These are your principles, like your own personal code of conduct. And you have some values around personal attributes. These are your essential character, to be applied in achieving your vision.

For example: Let's say your ultimate desire is a comfortable life and when you envisage yourself being comfortable, part of that is having financial security. Now, because you are an honest person, you don't go out and rob a bank to amass the money you want to secure your lifestyle! What you do to achieve your dream is use your ambition in building a rewarding career.

Have you ever felt the need to change something about yourself, your life, or your world? Clear values give you the courage and compassion to make choices about what you will attempt to change and what you'll learn to live with. Through open-ended questions asked respectfully, acceptance rather than judgement and reflective listening mentoring conversations invite the self-exploration that can reveal a person's values and make decision-making easier.

Values and Conflict

Values can influence the amount of conflict in your life.

Have you ever felt an inner conflict? Wrestled with your conscience? Taken a decision or choice that made you feel very uncomfortable? Felt unable to decide? Been pulled in different directions? Said one thing but done something else? Chances are you have and it's most likely because of a conflict of values within yourself.

Have you ever felt forced by people, circumstances, or immediate needs to act in ways that go against the grain? Maybe you want to do a task properly, thoroughly and to your own high standards, but there's a demand that you deliver results in too short a time frame for that, so you have to cut corners. Perhaps you have over-committed yourself and found yourself juggling many demands. Maybe you've operated under a stress level that affects on your efficiency and effectiveness. These are all examples of values in conflict. Often, interpersonal conflict is also a result of a clash of values.

Values and Priorities

Values determine your personal priorities - what you'll spend time or money on, what tasks take precedence over others, whose needs you will try to satisfy, and who you will ignore.

Sometimes people have a clash of values. I remember one time I was coaching a senior executive who wanted to talk about his work-life balance. He said he was worried because he didn't spend enough time with his little daughter and his wife was expecting another child. He talked about what he did on weekends, including mowing lawns and doing the edges. The simple solution, it seemed to me, was to pay someone to do that and free up his time to spend with family. Not so fast! That's my value-judgement talking, not his! Therefore, don't rush into giving answers and advice! He told me how relaxing it was to tend the garden, how much satisfaction it gave him to see it mown, neat and tidy by his own physical work after a week of meetings, battles, paperwork and such. I could not dictate what he should do. That's not my right. What I could do was to reflect to him his dilemma and allow him to work it through. Seeing the dilemma clearly empowered him to consider what he wanted to do about it. We also brainstormed other ideas for him to find the time he wanted. Now he's empowered to make a decision that's right for him.

We make a lot of decisions without conscious consideration of values, and that is why, in a mentoring conversation, bringing values into focus is so helpful. Clearly, values impact on your career decisions, life-style choices and the goals you select, pursue and achieve. Values affect your health and wellbeing, your material and financial situation, your relationships with other people and, most important of all, your relationship with yourself. So it's important to find out what your values are.

Values Clarification

Way to identify values:

1. Inventories, self-assessment instruments
2. Activities, simulations, exercises
3. Meditation
4. Interaction and experience
5. Observation and reflection
6. Guided conversation

Workshops and career counsellors may use the list approach, a values inventory, a more structured instrument, activities, simulations or exercises to elicit your values. One tool is the Career Values Card Sort[2] created by Richard Knowdell. In his book The Values Factor, Dr John Demartini offers a series of questions that allow us to use observation and reflection to identify our values. Kate Forster, in her beautiful book Spiritual Business, shares some helpful activities for identifying your values. Some people get deep insight from going within to tap their values through meditation.

Interaction with people and experience in your world constantly gives you information about your preferences, which are clues to your values. However, the bottom line is, regardless of the tool we use, we have to take time out to observe ourselves and reflect on our thoughts, feelings and actions, and this will allow us to identify values. A mentoring conversation can help you gain clarity about what is really important to you.

Examples of Values

Adventure, altruism, ambition, artistic creativity, authority, aesthetic beauty, belonging, challenge, compassion, community, competition, environment, excitement, fairness, family, forgiveness, freedom, friendship, fun, hard work, honesty, integrity, independence, influence, intellectual status, knowledge, learning, luxury, physical well-being, personal safety, power, recognition, respect, responsibility, security, service to others, spirituality, status, tradition, tranquility, variety, wealth, wisdom, work-life balance, world peace.

Questions that can stimulate values clarification:

- Who are your heroes or role models?
- What qualities do you most admire in them?
- What fires you up?
- What's most important to you?
- How would you spend your time if you didn't need to work?
- Describe a dream day?
- What do you do outside of work?

Activity
Look for more questions and use the Values Discovery Worksheet in the Mentoring Tools and Guides section of this book.

8

ON GOALS

I t's wise not to rush into goal setting.

According to thought leaders in mentoring, Clutterbuck and Megginson,[1] it's counterproductive to over-focus on goals too early in a mentoring relationship.

Mentees often come into a mentoring relationship with some ideas about what they might achieve. Sometimes their thoughts are quite specific and other times rather vague. Either way, the wise mentor will spend time helping the mentee to explore their ideas. When mentees reflect on what they want, explore with a mentor why they want it and how it aligns with values and strengths, they often realise that the original goal was a means to an end. It is the end result that is the actual goal that they are emotionally invested in.

EXPLORING a potential goal can be an enjoyable and satisfying conversation with a confidante, be they a mentor, friend, colleague or loved one. A reflective conversation can be framed by the acronym WISHES and may reveal:

- Wants—the heart's desire
- Importance—values, needs and drivers
- Strengths—personal attributes to build on
- Help—resources to draw on to achieve success
- Emotions and vision—a vividly imagined experience of success, and
- Strategies—what you'll do to move you towards these outcomes

Wants

Funnily enough, most of the time, we don't know what we want. We think we do and may be conscious, even fixated on some object or outcome, but, like the tip of an iceberg, a goal may be tangible and visible but superficial compared to what lies beneath. Aspirations are driven by heartfelt desires, subconscious needs, and values.

I'm not going Freudian on you here, just saying, put off writing goals until you've gone deeper. Self-reflection is vital and conversations with people who know how to listen stimulate just that.

Importance

Another reason to have company on this exploration is that they will notice when you "light up". In conversation, you'll become animated when you talk about the things that inspire you. Your passion becomes clear to others when you talk about what you love (or hate). You are energised and alive!

You may need a process to identify your values, work out any conflicting needs, and set priorities. Reflective listening by a mentor will help, and you'll find activities in the Mentoring Tools and Guides section of this book.

Strengths

Mentoring conversations create a safe space in which a mentee can speak about achievements, triumphs, and joys. Good questioning by mentors will expose and affirm the mentee's strengths. A mentor will ask questions like:

- What did you do?
- What came easily and naturally to you?
- How did you overcome challenges?
- What do you enjoy most?
- What are you good at?

There's a sweet spot where what a person is good at and what they love to do intersect. Richard Knowdell calls these "Motivated Skills". You have a high probability of success and satisfaction when you make using and developing Motivated Skills the focus of career planning. Knowdell has developed a card sort that helps identify motivated skills[2].

The late Donald Clifton, psychologist, author and chair of the global analytics and advice firm Gallup, has advanced the science of strengths. He wrote that every person has natural talents and when we invest in developing them; they become strengths. Gallup's book Discover Your Strengths[3] contains an access code to take the Top 5 Clifton Strengths Assessment.

Help

In my workshops, I often talk about the "wish list" and the "goal list". A wish list can be as long as you like. Nothing is too improbable to include, and all your hopes and dreams belong there. Your goal list should be short. You don't want too many active goals at any one time because that dissipates focus and energy.

Items from the wish list only make it to the goal list when a person is ready to commit the time, energy and resources to work towards them. Getting goals is difficult—otherwise we all would do it every time. There are obstacles, distractions and challenges along the way. So, before committing to a goal, a mentee needs to think about the help and support that will increase the likelihood of success. A mentor will ask:

- What do you need in terms of information or development to make this happen?
- What else might you need?
- How might you access that?
- Who are the people whose assistance or support might help?

Emotions and Vision

In order to capture and hold the powerful motivation to achieve an important goal, science has confirmed the power of vividly imagining yourself having achieved that result. A mentor might suggest or lead a visualisation process that a mentee can use daily. For example: "See yourself, looking out from your own eyes, with all the sensory richness you can. Feel the joy and satisfaction as you experience your success. Open your heart with gratitude and love to accept it."

Strategies

Of course, if you stop at setting a goal, visualising or even writing, the goal is all just dreaming. To get from where you are to where you want to be, you must move, change, become the person you visualise being. Strategies are, in broad terms, the steps you'll take to get there. The mentor will encourage the mentee to verbalise the goal and write a description of the desired outcome.

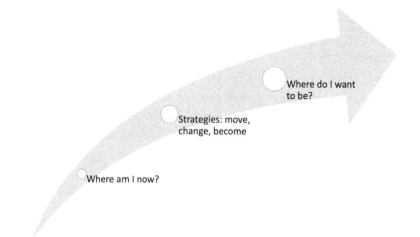

Obstacles and Barriers

Many people set goals and don't achieve them. Personally, I used to overload myself with too many goals. I have found myself with conflicting priorities that pulled me in different directions. There may be a difference between what you think you ought to do and what you really want to do. That is why clarifying values is important before you commit to goals. Activities such as Dartboard, The Clock and Values Discovery Worksheet in the Mentoring Tools and Guides section of this book will help.

When you set a goal, it's because you want to change. You want to move from where you are now to where you want to be. However, there is inner resistance to change because much of what we do is habit.

We all have unconscious patterns of behaviour. Similar to programs that run in the background on your computer, these operate in your brain like an auto-pilot, the default setting. That means you just get on with routine tasks with little need to think about them. It frees your conscious brain's power up to work on more challenging things. Because it takes effort and discipline to change, most of the time we revert to ingrained, automatic behaviour. Habits trumps discipline. Achieving a goal may mean:

- Learning new knowledge or skills
- Doing some things differently
- Changing habits

So it is important to discuss what needs to be done and how they can accomplish it. There is now scientific research into what works and what doesn't with setting and getting goals. Heidi Grant-Halvorson, of Harvard Business School, has published extensively on this topic, including her books: Succeed; how we can reach our goals, and 9 Things Successful People do Differently. Her findings are that to achieve your goals successfully, you need to:

1. Get specific
2. Seize the moment to act on your goals
3. Know exactly how far you have left to go
4. Be a realistic optimist
5. Focus on getting better rather than being good
6. Have grit
7. Build your willpower muscle
8. Don't tempt fate
9. Focus on what you will do, not what you won't do

Getting specific is critical, because if the goal is vague, it's easy to let yourself off the hook or give up when you're bored, discouraged or lazy. There's no messing with a clear, specific goal. It is job done, or not. Look at these vague New Year's resolutions. Is it any wonder that only 8% of people achieve such goals[4]?

Top Ten New Year's Resolutions

1. Improve Fitness
2. Eat better
3. Quit smoking
4. Quit drinking

5. Learn something new
6. Travel more
7. Volunteer
8. Meet someone
9. Sleep more
10. Get out of debt[5]

Most of us are over-scheduled and time-challenged. The combination of being "busy" and habits will defeat your good intentions if you don't seize the moment to act on your goals[6]. So you need to plan ahead and make time to take action. You can do this by creating "If... Then" rules. For example:

- I wake up early and I love to lie in bed and read a novel or go on Facebook. Now, I make it a weekend treat and instead: If it is 6am Monday to Friday, then I'm going to get up and exercise.
- I used to forget things in the supermarket. Now, as I think of things I need I add them to a list on my phone and, If I'm in the supermarket, then I'm using my list and buying only the stuff I need.
- I used to waste my best time ploughing through my inbox before I got started on "real work". So, If I'm at my computer first thing, then I'll set up my to do list and priorities for the day before I look at emails.

Heidi Grant Halvorsen's research shows that looking back at your progress can make it easy to become complacent. So, as you move forward, it is important to know exactly how far you have left to go. So you want to plan what you can monitor to track progress, AND have a way to see what's left. Decide how often you'll check and set reminders on your calendar. I recently used a weight loss app that showed my progress on a graph and showed the percentage of my goal I'd achieved. It was very satisfying to see the graph going down and the percentage going up - it also showed how much I had to go (I'm pleased to say I got 100% of my goal and then some).

To get your goals, you need to be a realistic optimist7. Expect the best, but plan for the worst. Belief that you can achieve your goal is a predictor of success. Believing it will be easy has the opposite effect. Over-confidence, or underestimating the challenge, works against goal achievement. A goal that is a stretch will take quite a lot of work. So think realistically about possible setbacks, things that could hold you back. Then figure out what you'll do if they occur. Consider the strengths you can apply and remember how you've overcome challenges in the past.

Some people think that ability is fixed. You are good at some things and not others. While you have natural talent and have a predisposition to develop strengths in some areas, that does not stop you from improving performance in others. In Mindset [7]Dr. Carol Dweckshows that effort makes a difference and when we are learning something new, we should acknowledge incremental improvement. So set goals for progress, not perfection, then take small steps because consistent and continual development means success. New tasks, outside your comfort zone or current ability, inevitably increase the likelihood of mistakes. Yet when people feel they are allowed to make mistakes—and learn from them — they actually make less[8]! So give yourself permission to stumble a bit in the beginning. And reach out to people who can help. Heidi Grant Halvorsen says that we should focus on *getting better* at something rather than *being* good at it.

Determination, commitment, and persistence are predictors of goal completion, but self-doubt can rob us of the grit to see the task through. Adopt a growth mindset, the belief that you can become stronger, that you can increase your ability, you can learn new skills and gain new knowledge and that with practice and experience, will improve performance.

Just as you wouldn't run a marathon without a long period of training, you can't imagine you can just decide and do all the things necessary to make a big change without preparation. You need to build your willpower muscle[9]. Like a muscle, willpower needs exercise to become strong. Choose slight challenges that are a bit of a stretch and build from there. Like a muscle, willpower gets tired. When you are tired, everything is harder. So timing is important. So is re-energising, rest and reward.

Don't take on too many willpower testing challenges at once. When you are trying to change, your habits will kick in, you'll revert to the old default behaviour easily in the early stages. Change your environment to support the new behaviour and avoid temptation. If you are giving something up it is easier to go without entirely than resist after a little – think chips and chocolate, can you stop at one? Heidi Grant Halvorsen warns "don't tempt fate".

When you try to *not* do something your focus is on that thing. Your attention is on that thing. Habits are hard to break because neural pathways in your brain are strong. Like computer memory, you usually can't completely wipe them but you can over-write them. Heidi Grant Halvorsen says: "focus on what you will do, not what you won't". So choose a *better* habit to substitute, something different and productive that you will do instead.

Michael Bungay-Stanier in his YouTube video *Building Rock Solid Habits*[10] describes using ABC as a formula for changing habits that don't serve you. The B stands for the old habit, behaviour that you want to change. Before B comes A, something that activates the behaviour. When does it happen? What set's you off? What circumstances trigger it? C is to decide on a new habit, something you will do instead. It needs to be quick (60 seconds or less) and easy.

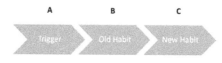

Goal Map

To achieve any important goal, you need an action plan. I have created the Goal Map that becomes an at-a-glance road map of your goal. It will help keep you motivated and on track. It's a visual reminder for continuous, consistent progress.

Goal Map

How to use the *Goal Map* is spelled out in the Guide to Setting and Getting Goals in the Mentoring Tools and Guides section of this book. Discussion of the questions it contains will ensure that a mentee:

1. Sets a goal they can commit to
2. Has an action plan for achievement
3. Considers obstacles and barriers and has strategies to deal with them

Activity for Mentees:

1. *Complete Dartboard and The Clock in the Tools and Guides section.*
2. *Take some time to reflect on these activities*
3. *Decide what you will put on your Wish List and what belongs on a Goal List*
4. *Select one goal that you are prepared to work on within your mentoring.*
5. *Work through the Goal Map with your mentor*

Activity for Mentors:

1. *Get very familiar with the activities above (the best way is to do them for yourself)*
2. *Prepare to facilitate productive, reflective conversations that lead the mentee through the goal mapping process*

PART III

MENTORING MINDSET

9

MENTORING MINDSET

One thing I've learned is that there's something beyond learning the techniques that make mentoring work. Skills and techniques are important, however, a mentoring mindset is just as valuable. The mentoring mindset includes the essential attitudes, values, or philosophy with which people approach their role in mentoring.

Having a philosophy of life, or principles that guide you, means that it's easy to make your own decisions without a lot of rules or instructions.

Over the years, I've observed the mindset that helps people get the most from mentoring conversations and relationships. It is one that values:

1. Courage
2. Being Constructive
3. Difference and Diversity
4. Responsibility
5. Dialogue

Courage

FOR MENTORS, it can take courage to accept the paradox of the role. You offer your ideas and experience and seek to inspire your mentee yet, encourage them to make their own decisions, knowing that their choices may not be the ones you'd make. For mentees, you make a courageous choice every time you divulge your aspirations, goals or obstacles and difficulties.

Both mentor and mentee may find that their assumptions and normal way of interpreting the world are challenged as they gain different ways of looking at things.

Both mentor and mentee need to have the ability to give and receive feedback. It takes courage to do both. You'll find ideas for giving and receiving feedback effectively in a later chapter.

To get the best from mentoring, you need to step up and accept the challenges offered by this kind of relationship. Mentoring is a unique chance to look at yourself, honestly. It is an opportunity to open your mind, question your thinking, consider alternatives and choose. Mentoring can literally change your mind. Because it is an adventure into the unknown for both the mentor and the mentee, it may be a bit scary.

Prepare and feel confident before you jump into mentoring. Mentoring involves creating a safe space for your conversations. This means building trust in one another. Agreeing and respecting confidentiality is a must.

Activity for Mentors

You need to make mentoring safe and yet be able to challenge mentees and make them think. In what ways will you do that?

Activity for Mentees

Mentees, you may be challenged to move out of your comfort zone. How will you deal with that?

Being Constructive

Mentoring is constructive. It empowers people to achieve outcomes they want. It allows them to be open to possibilities and explore options.

One way to ensure that mentoring conversations are constructive is by using Appreciative Inquiry. David Cooperrider[1] defines Appreciative Inquiry as:

"The cooperative search for what is best in people, their organizations and the world around them. It involves a systematic discovery of what gives a system "life" when it is most effective and capable in economic, ecological and human terms"

Mentoring utilises Appreciative Inquiry when mentors help mentees to recognise and value the best in themselves, situations, and other people. Together, they explore, discover, question and find new potential and possibilities. I've included some questions based on Appreciative Inquiry, the Guide to Questioning, in the Tools and Guides section of this book.

Jacqueline Stavros[2] and colleagues advocate building a strengths-based strategy in organisations and individuals and use the acronym SOAR (Strengths, Opportunities, Aspirations and Results) as an alternative to SWOT (Strengths, Opportunities, Weaknesses and Threats) in strategic planning. The acronym makes it easy to remember and SOAR is constructive in mentoring where what you want to do is:

- Identify and build on the mentee's strengths;
- Discover opportunities that mentees want to pursue;
- Clarify the mentee's aspirations in terms of personal values and vision; and
- Develop strategies and plans that produce results that are fulfilling to the mentee.

You'll find a list of sample questions based on SOAR in the *Guide To Questioning*, in the Tools and Guides section of this book.

Some people worry that being constructive by concentrating on strengths and opportunities means ignoring weaknesses and threats. It doesn't. You give an appropriate amount of focus to weaknesses, but reframe them—look at them from a more positive point of view —by including them in conversations about opportunities and results. Consider them as situations that the mentee can change. Because of that, weaknesses and threats become less demoralising and draining to talk about. You'll find the conversation more energising and enjoyable and goal oriented.

Marcus Buckingham and Donald Clifton[3] offer an extremely constructive approach to development in their book, *Now, Discover Your Strengths*. They recommend that each of us "become an expert in finding and describing and applying and practicing and refining our strengths", rather than focusing on weaknesses. They point out two popular but flawed assumptions. The first, that anyone can learn almost anything. The second is that our greatest potential growth lies in our areas of greatest strength. While sometimes a skills gap needs to be closed and competence gained through training, Buckingham and Clifton have shown that it is more correct to assume that each person's talents are enduring and unique and the greatest potential for growth is in the areas of our greatest strength.

I commend their book to you because it details an approach to developing yourself and those you may mentor. It also provides a mechanism that allows you to find out where you have the greatest potential for strength. When you buy the book, you get access to an on-line Strengths Assessment. This allows you to identify your most dominant themes of talent and the most potent areas for development.

The research of Dick Knowdell,[4] identified that when you use skills you are good at and enjoy, you are more likely to have career satisfaction and success and are less susceptible to stress and burnout on the job. He has a useful tool called the *Motivated Skills Card Sort* to help you identify your peak performance and development potential and the danger areas for burnout.

The thing that Appreciative Inquiry, SOAR, Now Discover Your Strengths and Motivated Skills all have in common is that they help you look for what works well and use that. It is very energising and inspiring when you do, and it gets the best results. This is important because of what we now understand about positivity.

Scientific research has advanced what we know about the influence of states of mind. Barbara L. Fredrickson Ph.D.,[5] in her book *Positivity*, shows that the difference between those who flourish and those who languish in life is the amount of positivity compared to negativity in their lives.

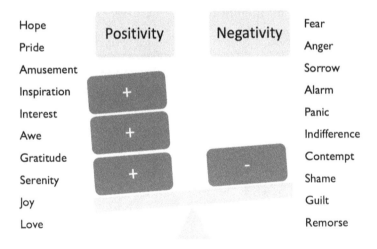

Positivity:Negativity

Positivity is not simply affirmations, positive thinking, or feel-good daydreams. It is increasing heartfelt positive emotions such as joy, gratitude, serenity, interest, hope, pride, amusement, inspiration, awe and love. Positivity has been shown to transform people and help them become their best. Mentors will improve their own lives, as well as those of their mentees, by increasing positivity in conversations.

Many years ago, I was facilitating a mentoring program for a government department. It included a series of regular half-day career development workshops attended by both mentors and mentees. They looked at their values, strengths, and career preferences. Not long after the program started, a new government was elected. The department was subjected to a sudden and dramatic change. There was turmoil, uncertainty and people were very anxious about their future. The mentoring program itself was threatened with termination. Fortunately, they allowed it to continue and at the conclusion, the entire group got together to celebrate. Mentors, as well as mentees, were grateful for the positivity of the program during such a period of negativity. One person described it as "like being in the eye of a storm, calm. A place where I could focus on myself and what I wanted, rather than being tossed about in turbulence."

Some ways that mentoring can increase positivity for both mentors and mentees are:

- Focusing on positive outcomes—discussing what the mentee wants, what they prefer, envisioning what the ideal situation would look like.
- Acknowledging differences between the current reality and an ideal situation.
- Drawing from past experience, evidence of strengths and strategies that work.
- Recognising what is within the mentee's power to change.
- Creating an action plan to take the steps that the mentee is willing and able to do.

Positivity doesn't mean being blind to negativity, wearing rose-coloured glasses or being foolishly optimistic. It means being realistic while maintaining the optimum positivity/negativity ratio.

It can be very positive for people to vent their negative emotions. Mentors can keep this type of conversation positive simply by listening attentively and with empathy. Often, we literally need to get something "off our chest" and a good listener is all we need to move into a more positive frame of mind. Sometimes, a mentor may feel that the mentee is sliding into self-pity, blame, excuses, or denial. A positive approach is to listen attentively, then shift the focus from the past or present reality to the desired future outcomes and what it would take to move in that direction.

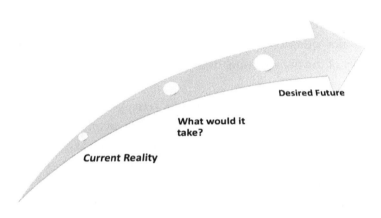

Shift the focus from past or present

A mentor of mine once said: "Be careful who you let in your mind". Be wary of overloading on violent TV, news or other messages that predict of doom and gloom. Take an audit of your media consumption. Aim for more positivity there, too!

Activity: Being Constructive

1. *Take the Positivity Self Test at* www.PositivityRatio.com
2. *Monitor your own thoughts for positivity and negativity. Play with adding more positivity to your day.*
3. *Based on what you want in the next three, six, or twelve months, list your own strengths, opportunities, aspirations, and results.*

Difference and Diversity

Workplace mentoring is unique because it sets aside any hierarchical status, such as management levels, and allows people to engage as equals, as adults, as professional colleagues. Yet, being equal does not mean being the same.

The greatest strength of mentoring is being partnered with someone different from you. Developing a relationship with someone you might not otherwise meet, someone older or younger, from another part of the organisation, or in some other way different from you, expands your thinking.

Noreena Hertz[6] explains that scientific research is now showing us that difference, dissent and discordant ideas actually make us smarter. If we can overcome our own discomfort and defensiveness and really hear a different perspective, we can bring more intelligence to decision-making.

Mentoring builds the confidence to acknowledge differences and respectfully disagree. It reduces resistance and defensiveness and allows people to explore ideas dissimilar to their own. This can produce more harmony, creativity, and productivity. But it relies on mutual respect.

When you have courage, you can develop a mentoring relationship that allows you to connect meaningfully and at a deeper level than you might with different people. There can be an honesty that allows you to share more of your thoughts and feelings in a mentoring conversation. You not only connect with the other person, but, perhaps more importantly, with yourself. You may discover and strengthen values, clarify preferences and understand your own motivation better.

It is easy to build connectedness with someone similar. Rapport is natural with people very like you. However, if you want to connect with others, you need to value differences. That means shifting from resistance to curiosity, being willing to listen and explore instead of fighting to hold your own position as superior. You need an open mind.

This doesn't mean giving up your beliefs! However, it does mean owning your values and opinions for what they are. Around any table, whether it's in a café, a home or a boardroom, people will have different beliefs about the same topic. Beliefs might be based on experience, the teaching of others, or speculation. Who is to say which belief (if any) is true? Each person thinks theirs is true, otherwise they wouldn't hold it. However, by definition, a belief doesn't have to be true or false—it's a belief! What gets us in to trouble is insisting our own belief is true and those of others are false.

Likewise, with opinions, there are people who make statements as if they were facts, when in fact, they are giving opinions. Mentoring asks us to sort fact from opinion and unmask assumptions.

Values are beliefs and opinions that motivate behaviour and decisions. Values help us determine what we think is right or wrong, good or bad, worthwhile or not worthwhile. It is rare for two people to have exactly the same values, though they may share some.

Our environment influences beliefs, opinions and values, experience, and exposure to information. Some views are based on limited horizons, unfortunate circumstances, misinterpretations, or inaccuracy. Mentoring is an ideal venue to explore values, beliefs and opinions so that the mentee can make informed choices congruent with what's most important to them.

Mentoring is supposed to be non-judgmental. Actually, that's a pretty impossible goal. Human beings are biologically programmed to make judgments every waking minute of the day. From pre-historic times, those who survived were the ones who could quickly decide: friend or foe? Good to eat or poison? Fight or flee? In mentoring, the best you can do is to suspend judgment. Just put it on hold for the duration of a conversation.

It's useful to name beliefs and opinions for what they are. Prefacing statements with phrases like: "I believe...", "I think...", "I feel...", "in my experience, what I have found is...", or "my view is...", flag that you are stating your own perspective. It also signals that you are open to the fact that others may have different ideas.

Each individual is unique. You may be of a different background, race, gender, age, or belief system to your mentoring partner. Yet, in mentoring, people become allies. There is a common purpose and you work together. You do not have to agree with each other's point of view. You don't have to change or adopt new beliefs. Simply respect differences and look at the value they add.

Activity: Difference

1. *Use the metaphor of a knife and fork to describe the value of differences (you might start by comparing the strengths and usefulness of each implement).*
2. *Make a list of how you and your mentoring partner differ.*
3. *Describe how you and your mentoring partner could capitalise on these differences.*

Responsibility

A mentor provides information, shares their experience, or expresses an opinion. However, it is always the mentee that decides, acts, and produces outcomes.

That said, a mentor has a duty of care. If the mentee proposes a course of action that the mentor can see is dangerous, the mentor should make the mentee aware of possible consequences. It takes courage and skill to have such conversations, and it requires an attitude of responsibility. The mentee is 100% responsible for their decisions and actions. The mentor's responsibility ends with doing their best to ensure that the mentee makes informed decisions about what can work for them in their situation.

There are boundaries to the mentor's role. At times, mentees may bring up problems that are outside the scope of the mentoring role and which the mentor is not equipped to deal with. It is important that both parties recognise the limitations of the mentoring responsibilities. When a mentor is not qualified to offer advice, they must refer the mentee to other sources. In the workplace, there are usually confidential avenues for assistance, and a mentor may do more harm than good by trying to help. If in doubt, have a confidential conversation with the Mentoring Program Co-ordinator, for guidance.

Activity: Responsibility

1. *Discuss why it is must be "always the mentee that decides, acts and produces outcomes" with your mentoring partner.*
2. *Review A Guide to Roles and Responsibilities, in the Tools and Guides section of this book.*
3. *Discuss with your mentoring partner.*

Dialogue

Mentoring is a two-way relationship, and it relies on a two-way conversation. Both parties need to develop listening and questioning skills so that actual communication occurs rather than superficial talk. Mentors and mentees must be present, attentive and focussed on understanding each other, not just waiting for their turn to speak.

Conversations where people express strongly held views that differ from your own can be extraordinary. The trick is to have a dialogue where emotion does not get in the way, where each really listens to the other with interest and respect. This is not a game of "agreeing to disagree". This is a conversation where agreement is irrelevant, where a joint decision is unnecessary and opinions do not have to match. Therefore, no one has to "win" or "lose".

If we were better at this kind of conversation, when we do have to reach an agreement or make a joint decision, the quality of the outcome and the relationship would be better. The problem is, few of us can practice such conversations. Mentoring is one place you can. Mentoring builds a relationship where you both express thoughts and feelings, facts and opinions in safety. A dialogue where people listen and are heard enables reflection before action. With a focus on outcomes, it encourages contemplation of consequences. This is why mentoring produces better decisions, goal achievement and life balance for mentees and mentors, too. They each become more skilled in the art of the mentoring conversation and transfer these skills into other workplace and personal relationships.

Dialogue is also important because human beings are very prone to errors of perception that often cause misunderstanding when people try to communicate.

One of my favourite movies, *Short Circuit*, features a robot "Johnny 5". Lightning strikes him and he "comes alive". He develops endearingly human capacities. Johnny 5 spends most of his time collecting, analysing and storing "input". He listens and watches 24 hours a day. Everything around him fascinates him, from a bird flying to kitchen appliances. His quest for input is insatiable. He speed reads everything available and finally discovers television. From the time you were born, "input", external and internal stimuli have surrounded you. There is more input than the processing capacity of your brain. Therefore, the brain's management systems take over to prevent overload. The first line of defence against overload is deletion.

Deletion is where the brain simply ignores information that seems unimportant, selecting instead those aspects that appear worthy of attention. For example, two people are having a conversation some distance away. You are not listening to it, you are merely aware of it in the background. Suddenly you hear your name mentioned and you "prick up your ears". Anyone who has had children is very familiar with the selective deafness they can exhibit. In a moment, stop reading and focus on all the sounds of which you were not aware whilst your attention was on reading. Pick a colour - any colour - and look around your environment. How many objects of that colour can you now see? Do the same with a particular shape - how many round objects are there? If you are sitting, now notice the sensation on your bottom, your thighs, back. Were you conscious of these sensations before? Strong sensory perception - physical discomfort, a loud noise, sudden movement - demands attention. But we normally reserve attention for a narrow band of sights, sounds and feelings, at the expense of others that are screened from perception. This means your brain deletes information before it even enters the awareness.

Deletion serves as a filter and allows the attention to be concentrated. However, placing the attention on some things means that others are missed. Attention is like the beam of a torch; it lights up and makes visible a small portion of the environment but by so doing renders the rest invisible or unclear.

The brain also deletes information from the short-term and long-term memory. Unless you consciously try to memorise information, details and events, it is only the high impact and meaningful that are remembered. Have you ever forgotten the name of a person seconds after they were introduced?

After an armed hold-up, police ask witnesses to complete written descriptions of the offenders without discussing the appearance of the robber with other people. Descriptions will vary significantly. Three people may see the same thing, hear the same speech, or take part in the same experience, yet have completely different perceptions. It is as if we filter perception through a series of lenses composed of preconceptions and past experience. Because deletion has already filtered out some aspects, the mind fills in the gaps with remembered or imagined data that fits the context. This is called distortion.

Distortion can prevent the discomfort of having to change preconceived ideas or face distressing truth. Such misrepresentation confirms cherished beliefs and reinforces ingrained attitudes. Galbraith[7] put it this way:

"Faced with a choice between changing our mind and proving that it is not necessary to do so, most of us will get busy finding proof."

Our brain's natural tendency to distort perception to make it fit what we already "know" means we need to work at having an open mind. We need to know that often what we think we hear is not what was said.

People can learn from experience because of their ability to **generalise**. Having learned to drive one type of car, a person usually has little difficulty driving another. If they wanted to drive a bus, their experience with cars would help. If you once tried eating an oyster and found it disgusting—or delicious—you could generalise that you will always find oysters disgusting or delicious. But what if you looked at an oyster and thought it looked disgusting and never tasted it? You might generalise that because it looked disgusting, it would taste disgusting, but you'd never know. A natural and useful tendency to generalise means that we need to develop a habit of questioning generalisations. When you hear a word like: *always, never, everyone, or nobody* it may be a generalisation you should question.

Given these filtering mechanisms, it is no wonder that we sometimes make errors of perception. Conversation can provide a different viewpoint. You can reconsider aspects of a situation that you may have deleted or distorted. You may challenge inappropriate generalisations. Perceptions may change through dialogue.

Activity: Dialogue

1. *Think of a time when you have had a true dialogue with someone, a free and frank exchange of views where you both felt heard and understood, even though you might not have agreed.*
2. *What were the circumstances that enabled you to have this kind of conversation?*
3. *What would you do to replicate the ability to have this kind of conversation in mentoring?*

What all of this means is that your mentoring conversation needs your full and active attention as well as the skills and techniques described in Part IV of this book. However, you need to bring a courageous mindset that enables you to be constructive, respect and value difference and diversity, take responsibility and engage in dialogue.

10

STRENGTHS-BASED DEVELOPMENT

Strengths-based development has its origins in positive psychology when leaders in the field started looking at what was *right* with people instead of what was *wrong* with them. Instead of "fixing" a deficit, the focus is on building capabilities.

Strengths-based development is used by coaches in all aspects of life to enable people to achieve their potential. It is also an approach now used in social work and disability, where counsellors and advocates build on what clients *can* do rather than their limitations. Strengths-based development in the workplace is valuable for individuals, teams and organisations.

The Foundations of Positive Psychology

Positive psychology emerged towards the end of the 1990s, fostered by Martin Seligman, then President of the American Psychologists Association. His studies in learned helplessness led him to add to the self-help field with books like *Learned Optimism*[1] and *Flourish*[2]. Another founder of positive psychology is Mihaly Czikszentmihalyi, who researched and wrote about the experience of flow [3]and how it can be achieved. Donald O. Clifton studied successful individuals to discover what they did right. He developed strengths-based psychology[4], finding that different people used their different natural strengths to achieve that same excellent results.

Carol Dweck's work with mindset [5]has shown teachers, parents and business people the value of a growth vs fixed mentality and, Barbara Fredrickson has led the way in using positivity[6] to build resilience and well-being.

Why Use a Strengths-based Approach?

In recent years, there has been a shift in the approach to Performance Management[7]. Research has shown that tick-the-box and ratings-based performance reviews say more about the rater than the ratee. It may be a feel-good exercise for some, but for others it can be a back-ward-looking, weakness-focussed, punitive approach that costs a lot and does nothing to improve performance. Strengths-based development changes that.

As organisations have moved to capability frameworks, we've found that developing capability fits very well with a strengths-based approach that encourages employees to take responsibility for developing their potential and productivity.

Managers always want to know how to motivate employees, but now we know that there is less need to motivate people when they are engaged. People who are engaged love their work, speak positively about their organisation, and perform above and beyond expectations. They are emotionally and intellectually committed to the organisation—in other words, you have captured their hearts and minds. A strength-based approach develops engagement.

One of the most productive applications of strengths-based development is building team effectiveness. Understanding individual strengths and differences, complementary and dynamic combinations with team-members and the strengths of the team itself is empowering.

For a leader, understanding your own strengths and those of the people you lead is essential. Your role is pivotal in team effectiveness, engagement, building capability and performance management because 70% of the variability in employee engagement is down to the relationship with the immediate boss.

Working with people to build strengths improves relationships and engagement. So, you owe it to yourself to take on strengths-based development.

Business Benefits from Strengths-based Development

A global study of ROI by Rigoni and Asplund[8] found:

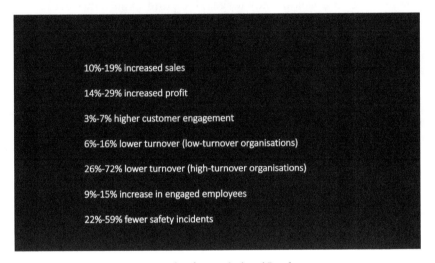

10%-19% increased sales

14%-29% increased profit

3%-7% higher customer engagement

6%-16% lower turnover (low-turnover organisations)

26%-72% lower turnover (high-turnover organisations)

9%-15% increase in engaged employees

22%-59% fewer safety incidents

Business Benefits of Strengths-based Development

There are tremendous advantages for individuals who build and use their strengths. There's something within us that calls us to develop natural talents and there is joy in answering that call. It invigorates you when you use your strengths. Learning is quicker, easier, more enjoyable and you are more engaged and likely to experience "flow". Excellent performance is fulfilling. People who use their strengths every day are 12.5% more productive. That means you get more done working no harder. All of this feels good and makes you feel strong. When you are strong, you can take challenges in your stride, you are less susceptible to stress. And the bottom line is, when you are the best you can be, you contribute the most to work, life, community and the world.

Gallup's research has found that People working with their strengths look forward to going to work, have more positive than negative interactions with co-workers, treat customers better, tell their friends they work for a great employer, achieve more on a daily basis and have more positive, creative and innovative moments.

Coming from a learning and development perspective, we used to think that when there was a difference between a person's performance and the level of performance required of them, what they needed was to develop knowledge, skills and experience. Later, we realised that often teaching people what to do and how to do it and even coaching and supporting their practice, does not necessarily transfer to better performance on the job. We need to look at factors within and outside the person that cause them to want to deliver the desired performance. The external factors are down to management; the internal we might call intrinsic motivation.

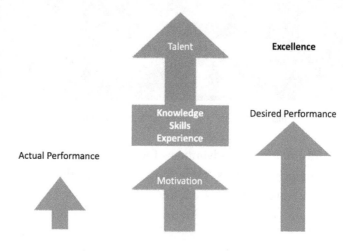

Performance Discrepancy

Most people who want to can work hard, learn and practice so that they reach an acceptable standard in the role we have hired them for. If they can't, you need to reassess your recruitment and selection process. However, excellence in any field is more likely to be achieved by those who have and develop a natural talent for it. Most of us can run, but few will ever become champion runners. Many can write, yet scarcely any are best-selling authors. Everyone can do simple addition, but a minority are mathematicians. Talents usually mean that we have a natural predisposition for something and enjoy it so much we do it frequently enough to become good at it.

"No one excels at everything,
but everyone can be great at something".

The University of Nebraska did one of the early studies[9] that prompted strengths-based development was done by. They set out to improve the speed-reading skills of students and measured results over 3 years. Over 1,000 students were tested for speed and comprehension. At the beginning, average readers achieved 90 words per minute, while above average readers could do 350 words per minute. All learned effective reading techniques, and all improved. However, while average readers made a modest improvement from 90 WPM to an average of 150WPM, outstanding results were achieved by those who were already fast readers who started at 350WPM and achieved a staggering 2900 WPM.

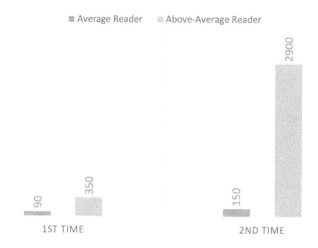

■ Average Reader   ■ Above-Average Reader

Reading Study University of Nebraska

What this shows is that in areas that we are weak, we can work hard, learn techniques and improve, but where we are strong the opportunity for improvement skyrockets.

Strengths-based development can be difficult if we hang on to the popular, but incorrect, notion that we should concentrate on improving weaknesses. Research shows we should not ignore some weaknesses, but we are more productive, engaged, and satisfied when we develop and use our strengths. Continued research[10] into investing in strengths development as opposed to trying to fix weaknesses found it takes about the same amount of effort to improve -10 to -4 as is it does to improve +10 to +40.

To excel, we need to focus on strengths and manage weaknesses. That means being aware of areas of weakness that are requirements of our role. Then deciding when to work hard to bring our performance to the required standard and when to work around them by delegating, outsourcing, partnering, systemising or automating tasks. Gallup says:

"Weakness-fixing prevents failure;
Strengths-building leads to success."

How Well do You See Your Strengths?

Some strengths you'll be aware of. Others recognise these in you, too. These are your confirmed strengths. You'll also know some areas where you are not strong and others would agree. You need to manage these because they are potential stumbling blocks. Unfortunately, we can't always see our strengths or our weaknesses. You have unrecognised strengths—others see them, but you are unaware. When it's pointed out, you are likely to say: "anyone could do it" or "doesn't everyone do that?" Because a skill comes naturally and easily to you, you may take it for granted. There will also be areas that others see, but you don't, where you're *not* strong. We all have blind spots. So it is important to seek and to be open to feedback.

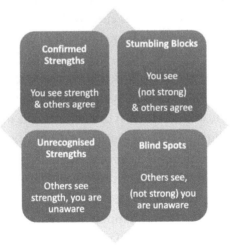

How well do you see your strengths?

What Are Strengths?

Some things come easily and naturally to us, others don't because we have a natural talent for certain things, the right ingredients that come with the package of our body, brain and personality.

Talent is your pre-disposition, the raw material, a natural part of your personality. You are born with talents and they stay with you throughout life.

You build talents into strengths by adding **knowledge, skills, and experience.** Like building a muscle, you must use knowledge and practice skills to become strong.

Knowledge is information you gain and understand. You recall it when you need to, or internalise it so that you use it without even thinking about it.

Skill is the ability you develop, the techniques you learn, the know-how that comes from practice.

Some of us have developed one or two strengths but as someone once said: "If all you have is a hammer, it's tempting to treat everything like a nail". So, what we want to do is see what other tools we have in the kit and learn how to use them. This is especially important in the dynamic and fast-changing workplace of today.

Strengths will generally fall into one of four categories:

1. **How you think about information and situations.** How do you mentally navigate your world? Do you have a focus on the future or an interest in the past? Like to analyse data or situations? Love learning, reflecting and drawing the lesson from events? Consume and absorb information, collecting facts and interesting ideas? Do you seek what you need to make better decisions?

2. **How you make things happen.** Are you a get-it-done type of person? Disciplined and focussed? Take responsibility? Fix things? Driven by a purpose? Good at organising others? Work out the steps? Pursue goals?

3. **How you influence others.** Do you take charge? Motivate? Compete? Communicate well? Are you self-confident? Persuasive? Always looking for improvement? Want to be known for some significant contribution?

4. **How you build and maintain relationships** Are you a people-person? Find it easy to empathise with others? Inclusive, making all feel welcomed? Flexible and able to

tailor your approach to a person's uniqueness? Love to help people develop? See the bright side of situations?

The Gallup[11] organisation has been researching effectiveness in the workplace for decades. It has defined 34 talent themes across these four areas as: Strategic Thinking, Executing, Influencing and Relationship Building. We benefit from all four domains in effective teams. Individuals may have dominant strengths in one, two, three, or all four.

How to Recognise and Develop Strengths

To turn talents into strengths, we need *opportunity*—the chance to develop. We also need to be willing to *invest* time and energy in building talents so they truly become strengths. That's why I say that I never met a person who did not have more potential and more to contribute. Often, we have not had the awareness or the opportunity, or we may not have invested in developing our strengths.

One way to develop an awareness of talents and strengths is through personal reflection; another is through feedback. A third is with a psychometric instrument. The best way is to combine all three.

I recommend a reflective journal. It will take some time, but can be extremely rewarding to write introspectively, putting your thoughts and feelings on paper. Here are some thought-starter questions you could reflect on:

1. What do you look forward to doing most at work?
2. Which activities do you complete quickly and easily?
3. What do you enjoy doing most outside of work?
4. What did you enjoy doing most in previous roles?
5. What do other people say you do best?
6. What are you known for?
7. What is your dream job? Why?
8. After living expenses, what do you spend your money on?
9. What did you love as a child?

10. What would friends and co-workers say were your talents?

These questions are great for a mentor to discuss with a mentee, but probably require some reflective thinking time for the mentee first.

Then this information can be used to pick up clues to talents and strengths. In terms of personality, do the answers reveal more of a doer, persuader, people-person or someone who loves information?

Online Strengths Assessment

The instrument I recommend for discovering talents and strengths and the one I use in coaching, mentoring programs and workshops is the CliftonStrengths Assessment. You can purchase this and do it online. It comes with detailed reports and a great deal of helpful information about using your results.

Once you have an awareness of talents and strengths, you can start to develop them using the 70:20:10 strategies described in chapter 4 Learning and Mentoring.

Activity: Identify Your Strengths

1. *Take the 30 Day Challenge: Every day, at least once a day, stop and reflect: **what did I do well?** Write it down, especially if you enjoyed it, especially if you felt strong when you did it!*
2. *At the end of 30 days, share your notes with a mentoring partner. Look for patterns and evidence of your strengths.*
3. *Invest in the Clifton Strengths Assessment here: www. gallupstrengthscentre.com*

11

COMMUNICATION STYLES FOR MENTORING

There are many communication styles, but two, the facilitative style and the authoritative style[1], originally described by Postle, are particularly effective in a mentoring relationship.

The Facilitative Style

- *Supporting*—attentive listening, affirming, empathy
- *Eliciting*—questioning, drawing out thoughts and feelings
- *Exploring*—developing and evaluating ideas and options

The Authoritative Style

- *Confronting*—objective feedback, challenging perceptions
- *Informing*—explaining facts, accessing resources, sharing experience
- *Guiding*—describing likely consequences of particular actions, suggesting, advising, recommending

Neither style is better than the other, but over-use of one or other can detract from communication. The two styles are complementary. Both are necessary for effective mentoring.

The **facilitative** style draws out what a person already knows. Both mentor and mentee use this style, at different times, to elicit information. It reveals tacit knowledge and creates the space for those "aha" moments of discovery and insight.

Don't confuse the **authoritative** style with authoritarian methods. The former is assertive, the latter aggressive. The authoritarian communicator states their opinions or beliefs as if they were facts; whereas you use the authoritative style to express your opinion or belief and own it as an opinion or belief.

The authoritative style uses phrases like "I think...", "I believe...", "My understanding is..." to show their statement is a theory, based on the speaker's own experience or logic.

Using the authoritative style allows a mentor to give the mentee vital feedback. If you do this in an assertive, not aggressive way, it is less threatening and therefore reduces defensiveness. When people are defensive, they tend to reject feedback, rationalise, give excuses or counterattack.

When there is rapport, trust and an effective relationship built on the facilitative style, it is easier to receive feedback, delivered in the authoritative style, without getting defensive.

Strong communicators can shift styles easily. A good mentor can switch from giving advice to eliciting information, or from challenging someone to being supportive. Or they can choose to be silent and simply listen, allowing the mentee to fully express themselves. When the mentee reflects on their feelings, and thoughts, or reviews events, they often discover their own answers.

The mentee uses the facilitative style to draw on the experience of their mentor and get input from them. The mentee uses the authoritative style to express themselves when they are reflecting. After all, they are the authority on their own experience.

Facilitative Skills

Supporting

- Affirming their worth
- Giving good attention
- Expressing care or concern
- Appropriate sharing & self-disclosure
- Encouraging celebration of personal attributes

Eliciting

- Provoking self-discovery through reflection
- Asking clarifying questions
- Prompting to say more
- Using reflective listening to help someone express their feelings

Exploring

Asking questions that help:

- Generate options and possibilities
- Evaluate the pros and cons of options or actions
- Consider consequences of decisions before action is taken

Authoritative Skills

Confronting

- Giving feedback
- Challenging perceptions

- Describing how others may perceive a situation or behaviour

Informing

- Imparting information
- Expressing your perception
- Sharing your own experience
- Giving your opinion or stating your point of view
- Explaining
- Providing background
- Identifying other resources

Guiding

- Describing possible consequences of a particular action
- Suggesting
- Advising
- Recommending

Personal Style

Your mentoring needs to be a balance of facilitative and authoritative styles. Yet most people have a natural tendency to be better at, or more inclined to use, one style rather than the other.

For some, the authoritative style does not come easily. We like to be liked and sometimes avoid confrontation. But being nice to people and tiptoeing around their feelings can be a disadvantage in a mentoring relationship, where learning and growth is the aim.

On the other hand, the sensitivity, patience and trust called for by the facilitative style can be a challenge. We may be expected to be direct, decisive problem solvers in the workplace. The authoritative style may be a habit.

Both styles are worth developing and both styles have benefits that go beyond mentoring. Leadership, parenting, friendship, in fact, almost any interpersonal relationship, can benefit from the balanced use of the facilitative and authoritative styles of communication.

Activity: Communication Styles

1. *List the advantages and disadvantages of the authoritative and facilitative style.*
2. *Which style comes more easily/naturally to you?*
3. *Can you switch freely from one style to another?*
4. *What could be the disadvantages of over-use of your favourite style in mentoring?*
5. *What benefits might there be in development greater strength in the other style?*
6. *Who might give you objective feedback on your use of these styles?*
7. *How might you develop your use of a particular style or increase your flexibility in using the styles?*

PART IV
SKILLS

12

BUILD TRUST

W hat is it that allows us to trust someone? I believe there is a trust zone that is a culmination of several elements: credibility, reliability, mutuality and reciprocity.

Some of what opens our trust zone is emotional, and some is rational.

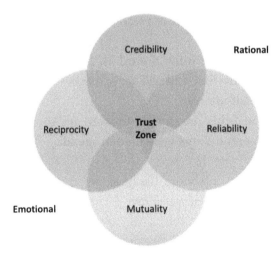

The Trust Zone

Those we consider trustworthy typically share some characteristics that allow them to establish **credibility** with us. We believe in their:

- Integrity—they are honest and congruent. They do not lie. Their words and deeds match, they "walk the talk". They act in alignment with the values they espouse.
- Capability—they have knowledge, skills, abilities that inspire our confidence. They know what they are talking about, their information is reliable. They have experience in their field.

We experience them as **reliable:**

- **Performance**—they produce results. Get things done. Do the right things that make for effectiveness. It is not enough to look good, they must fulfil the promise, meet expectations.
- **Consistency**—they turn up, meet commitments, do what they say they will, on time.

With people we trust, there is a sense of **mutuality:**

- Intent—they are positive toward us. They care about us, not just themselves, and will act in our best interests, not purely in self-interest.
- Motivation—they are straight-forward and their reasons are transparent. There is no hidden agenda.

Interestingly, you are more likely to get trust if you give trust. Trust is **reciprocated** when you show:

- **Respect**—you acknowledge me as a person, my intelligence and autonomy and my right to be treated as an adult

- **Confidence**—you show faith in my ability, believe I will do my part

So, trust is not something you have, or you don't. There are behaviours and skills that you can develop.

1. **Communication**—listening, questioning, non-verbal
2. **Feedback**—positive and genuine and, once you have established trust, corrective.
3. **Self-disclosure**—to help them get to know you as a person

I will address listening, questioning, feedback, and self-disclosure in the next three chapters.

MENTORING IS A UNIQUE RELATIONSHIP. Regardless of their age, or role in an organisation, both parties come to the mentoring relationship as adults and equal partners. Their aim is to communicate openly, sharing ideas, thoughts, and feelings.

Most mentoring programs will have the pairs agree to confidentiality and many will have their own version of the *Mentoring Code* that I've included in the Tools and Guides section of this book. Discussing these types of ground rules helps to build a foundation for the trust and respect that will make a mentoring relationship work.

Emotional Reactions

Trust activates the prefrontal cortex. This part of the brain enables you to make reasoned decisions (often referred to as the executive function). When engaged, the executive function can regulate your emotional reactions. However, emotions get out of the gate faster and are hard to catch - think tortoise and hares! Fatigue, hunger or stress increase the likelihood of emotional reactions that can hijack a rational response to events. Dr Dan Seigel calls this "Flipping your lid"[1]. If you flip your lid, you are temporarily out of control and cannot reason at all.

You can train yourself to pause and develop the habit of engaging your executive function. However, sometimes emotions still win. Perceived threat can lead to aggressive defensive and passive defensive actions.

In mentoring conversations, we need to use our skills intentionally and focus on constructive outcomes. Below, you can see typical defensive reactions (see more on defensiveness in chapter 13 Listen Well).

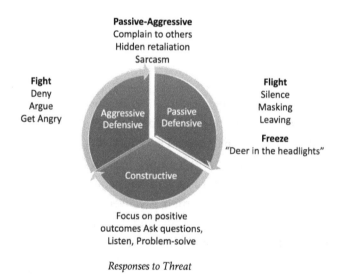

Responses to Threat

Most of us don't realise is the degree to which *any* interaction with others triggers emotions and defensive reactions. Anything perceived as a threat or reward causes the brain to respond.

Brains work differently when emotions cause various neurochemicals to flow. Dopamine is associated with pleasure and reward, oxytocin with bonding and love, cortisol, norepinephrine and adrenalin with stress.

Evolution has ensured that our brain's first function is to keep us safe physically and emotionally. Five times per second, the brain evaluates the environment for threat or reward. This is an automatic and usually non-conscious action as natural as breathing, designed to protect us from pain and move us toward pleasure. Humans would not survive without the brain's inbuilt threat/reward vigilance and systematic response.

A perceived threat activates a primal survival response—fight/flight/freeze. There are physical changes: heart rate and blood pressure, perspiration, digestion, blood sugar, all gearing our body for a burst of energy that will help us run away from the threat, fight it off, or freeze—hoping to be invisible.

Today we are rarely in situations where we literally have to fight or run for our lives, but it is easy to trip the threat switch—a look, a tone of voice, a word. The brain can't tell the difference between a genuine threat and an imagined one. Ever watched a scary movie and felt your heart thumping? Or nearly jumped out of your seat when the raptor leaped at you on-screen? Once fight/flight/freeze is primed, you stay jumpy for some time!

Real or imagined, threats in the work environment can range from a minor embarrassment to major, fear-inducing situations, like demotion or potentially losing your job.

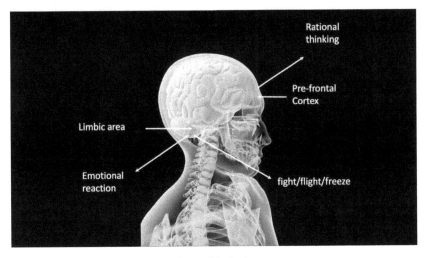

Areas of the Brain

Threat/Reward

Neuroscientist Evian Gordon[2] describes the **minimise danger/maximise reward** response as "the fundamental organising principle of the brain". This means that the brain automatically wants to avoid anything threatening. The flip side is that the brain is attracted to things it perceives as rewarding.

Dr. Norman Chorn and Dr. Terri Hunter of the BrainLink Group[3], have described five social drivers that stimulate the threat/reward response in the brain. They use the acronym SAFETY.

Security—certainty, predictability, stability
Autonomy—freedom to decide and choose
Fairness—equity, transparency, social justice
Esteem—status in relation to others, recognition
Trust—belonging to a group or tribe, feeling safe in relationships with others.
Your personal priorities within the five

Security

The brain conserves energy by running on automatic as often as possible. We use routines, habits, and the rules of thumb to make millions of minor decisions each day. Default settings allow us to do things without thinking. This way the brain minimises effort. Therefore, the brain hates change, disruption, and the unexpected. Switching off auto-pilot to use the executive brain to process new data and act deliberately, instead of out of habit, requires effort and uses vital energy. Security, to the brain, means routine, ordinary, no surprises. The need for security means that we experience ambiguity, confusion, or unmet expectations as a threat and become defensive. Familiarity, previous or similar experience, clear expectations, being prepared, forewarned, or briefed about expectations signal safety.

Autonomy

Adults want to be self-directing. Most of us hate rigid rules, being given orders or micromanaged. We resent top-down planning that robs us of input. It feels disempowering and will trigger the brain's defences. When we feel we are in control, have independence and choices, we can work in collaboration and feel safer.

Fairness

The perception of favouritism, preferential treatment, or arbitrary decisions will flick this switch to threat. Transparency, logical rationale for decisions, and equity reassures us.

Esteem

We instinctively understand the importance of status. High-status individuals get more. Whether it's food, money, sex, the corner office, the car or parking spot or better assignments at work.

The brain is constantly testing our status in relation to others. Feeling judged or looked down on, negative feedback, not winning in a competitive situation, lack of money or having to do the dirty work can lower self-esteem and raise defensiveness. Mastery—self-efficacy, seeing ourselves as competent, being treated with respect, being acknowledged, positive feedback and praise register in the brain as rewarding.

Trust

Rejection, isolation, loneliness, feeling different and socially disconnected are very threatening and cause great pain. Inclusion, being part of a group, rapport and empathy, feeling understood, friendship and belonging make us feel safe.

While all these drivers can trigger your brain's threat/reward response, there is usually one that is more dominant. For some, autonomy might be the number one driver, while a need for security compels others.

Your Dominant Driver

It's useful to know your dominant social driver because the one you find most important will be what you try to offer most to others. Unfortunately, if there is a mismatch—say I'm trying to offer you lots of autonomy and freedom (my preference), but you value security, clear guidelines and certainty, that could be a barrier in our relationship and communication.

The table below shows what mentors can do to minimise threat and maximise reward in terms of brain response.

Security, certainty, predictability, stability	Agreeing ground rules Discussing expectations Sharing an agenda prior to meeting
Autonomy, freedom to decide and choose	Listening and asking more Make their own decisions They take responsibility
Fairness, equity, transparency, social justice	See both sides of an argument Different perspectives Championing equity
Esteem, status in relation to others, recognition	Treat them as equal, not patronizing Slow to give advice, even when asked Positive feedback and/or get them to reflect and recall their own success
Trust, belonging to a group or tribe, feeling safe in relationships with others	Build rapport every time Be willing to disclose Show you trust them
Your dominant driver	Will filter your perception What you offer first may not match their needs

Ways Mentors can Apply "SAFETY"

Thinking Patterns

Your brain's threat response is a survival instinct to help us cope with life. However, it can cause defensive thinking that reinforces the threat, heightens tension and impedes communication and relationship building. The good news is that the opposite is also true. The more we engage the executive function of the brain, the more we can self-regulate. Mentors can help mentees do that.

To help others, we must start with ourselves. Remember what they say in the safety demonstration on an aircraft "fit your own mask before you try to help others". So, we must be able to model non-defensive behaviours and develop the habit of non-defensive thinking, if we are to assist others. That begins with recognising some thinking patterns that can put us into a vicious circle of defence or a virtuous circle of trust.

Catastrophising

One type of unhelpful thinking is catastrophising. This is where we worry about something and escalate it. We make a mountain out of a molehill; we turn a minor setback into a major catastrophe. We act as if the worst-case scenario is inevitable. Now remember, this type of thinking is generated by the fight/flight reaction. It's triggered by emotions—I call them E-motions because they provide energy to move us. We have evolved from survivors who thought of worst-case scenarios so they could run from them, fight them or freeze and hide from them. Today, that sometimes serves us, but most times it causes unnecessary fear and stress that can prevent us thinking clearly, eat up our energy and obstruct communication.

The alternative is to put things in **perspective.**

A helpful habit is to get your executive function (the rational decision-making part) on the case to regulate the emotional reaction. First, notice catastrophising thinking and ask:

"On a scale of 1-10, how likely is this to happen?"
And,
"On a scale of 1-10, how bad would it be if it did?"

As a mentor or friend, you can ask these questions too. Just make sure you have listened well, used empathy and allowed the other person to vent emotions before you use this technique to bring in their rational thinking. We are talking about building trust, so ignoring, devaluing, or over-riding someone's emotions will do the opposite.

Dichotomous Thinking

Dichotomous thinking is either/or, black and white, you're either for me or against me. Something is simply good or bad, right or wrong. There are no shades of grey, no nuance, no layers. However, our executive brain can entertain **possibilities**, seeing beyond black and white, unpacking the issue and exploring the complexities.

Surface Issues

Under threat, our vision is narrow and shallow. We see and react to the surface issue, especially in a conflict situation. The executive function can take us deeper, looking for **underlying needs** that help us understand different points of view. The executive function is behind active listening. Curiosity and respectful enquiry allow us to negotiate, problem solve and resolve conflict.

The Need to be Right

When it's us against the world, we need to be right! We want to prove we are correct. We marshal all arguments to defend our position. We may cherry pick facts, deny contrary evidence, dig our heels in and become more convinced or entrenched in a particular point of view. It takes a strong will and/or a practiced executive function to lose our fear of contradiction. Only when we feel secure, can we let go of the need to be right and be **willing to learn**—in fact change our mind.

Assumptions

We all do this from time to time, jump to conclusions based on limited information, mistake opinions for facts, pre-judge based on fear or limited experience, act as if beliefs were truth. You've heard people make statements, as if they were facts, when in fact they were stating an opinion. You've heard people claim something as the truth, when in truth it's a belief. There's nothing wrong with being true to your beliefs or having strongly held opinions; what gets us in to trouble is when we insist they are facts or truth. We set up conflict: If I am right, you must be wrong. If my belief is true, yours must be false.

There are two very constructive things we can do instead. One is to recognise and own beliefs, opinions and assumptions. Using statements like:

"I believe..."
"I think..."
"In my opinion..." or
"In my experience, what I've found to be the case is..."

A belief cannot be true or false—it's a belief. An opinion recognises that there are other points of view. Owning opinions and beliefs allows dialogue. **Critical thinking,** enabled by the executive function, interrogates assumptions, sorts facts based on science, research and actual experts, from opinion and respects beliefs for what they are - faith, in the absence of proof.

Self-justification

Confrontation or contradiction can be very threatening and cause the brain to spring to self-justification, excuses, or even denial. Have you noticed how hard it is for people to apologise? Media personalities who make sexist comments or who are called out on offensive remarks and sports people who bring the game into disrepute often make faux-apologies. Faux-apologies are along the lines of "if people were offended, I'm sorry" instead of an unqualified "I acted thoughtlessly and I and I apologise". It is a bigger person who can **acknowledge** offence given and accept, not try to excuse their mistake.

If we want to reduce the threat response of the brain, reduce stress and lead conversations to constructive outcomes, we need to start to notice—not just in others but in ourselves—the thinking patterns and behaviours triggered by social drivers (SAFETY). Patterns of thinking are caught not taught, constructive thinking requires conscious effort and practice.

Here's another acronym of ideas to help mentoring partners build trust and an effective relationship:

TOGETHER—WE'RE in this together, we're partners, we're allies. We may be very different, but we've come together with a common goal to have conversations and interactions that will create positive outcomes.

RESPECT—WE listen to each other. We build rapport by finding what we have in common and we accept the inevitability that we are different, perhaps by gender, culture, age, experiences, beliefs or points of view. We accept we are free to hold and share our own opinions and different perspectives, and we have the right to disagree.

UNDERSTANDING—WE slow down our thinking, reducing hasty assumptions, conclusions or judgment. Instead, we explore context, and each other's reality. We use empathy to get a sense of what it might be like for each other. We enquire, we are curious, and we keep an open mind.

SUCCESS—WE share positive intention. We build a constructive relationship. We have a sense that our actions have the power to produce beneficial results. We set goals and work toward positive outcomes.

. . .

TALK—OUR conversation is purposeful. We create a safe space where we each can be candid and open to share thoughts and feelings. We can exchange views non-defensively. We discuss issues, problems and choices and decisions in confidence and respecting privacy. We collaborate to generate ideas, alternatives and possibilities. Communication is two-way and we give and receive honest feedback so we learn from each other.

Activity: Build Trust

1. *Identify which social driver is dominant for you.*
2. *Self-disclosure by both parties will build trust. So have a conversation about the SAFETY model.*
3. *Reflect on your dominant driver and that of your mentoring partner.*
4. *Discuss your similarities and differences.*

13

LISTEN WELL

"We have been given two ears and but one mouth, in order that we may listen more and talk less"
Zeno of Citium
Philosopher, Athens (300 BC)

L istening is important in all relationships. In mentoring, it's especially important that we show a willingness to really HEAR each other.

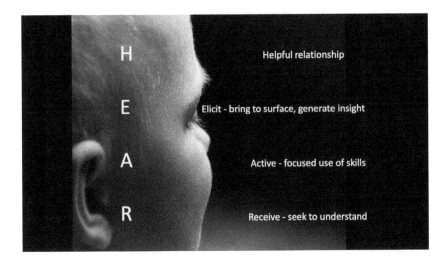

Mentors invite mentees to confide in them because they have committed to a helpful relationship. Whether it's focused on career development, support through challenges or speeding up growth and potential, mentoring depends on exceptionally good listening.

For a mentor, the purpose of listening is to elicit what the mentee has to say. To bring to the surface their thoughts and feelings, values and priorities and increase their ability to generate insight from the mentee's own experience so they can navigate a way forward.

For the mentee, listening is a vital tool for getting the most out of mentoring. It means being open to new ideas and different perspectives - no-one develops by staying the same. You always have the freedom to make your own choices, but if they are to be informed decisions, hearing input from others will help broaden your options.

Passive listening is lazy. Mentoring is active, and listening is a focused use of skills. It can be hard work, it doesn't necessarily come naturally, and it can be difficult—until you have practiced and practiced, so it becomes second nature.

The type of listening mentoring requires is one where we open ourselves to receive what the other person says and we seek to understand their perspective.

The Role of the Mentor

One problem for listening in mentoring, is misunderstanding the role of the mentor. The traditional view of mentoring is that of someone who imparts their wisdom, sharing their knowledge and experience. And, while that is useful, in contemporary mentoring a mentor does a lot more listening than talking.

First and foremost, a mentor's job is to elicit what's going on for the mentee. Excellent mentors ask a lot of questions before they ever offer an opinion. Mentees sometimes want opinions, suggestions and advice from mentors, but there are dangers with jumping in too fast (see chapter 5 Be Slow to Offer Advice).

Defensiveness

One thing we always have to be careful about is triggering defensiveness. Defensiveness gets in the way of communication and relationships. Mentoring takes a great deal of trust and openness, and building that takes time. As discussed in the previous chapter, Build Trust, defensiveness triggers neurological responses—the automatic fight/flight/freeze reaction. When someone gives advice, reactions can include:

- Fight—arguing, denial or getting angry
- Flight—changing the subject or opting out of the conversation
- Freeze—being unable to respond or even think

To communicate openly, we need to feel safe and let defences down. Listening well allows people to express themselves without fear.

What Does It Take to Really Hear?

"Most people do not listen with the intent to understand, they listen with the intent to reply."
Stephen Covey

In Stephen Covey's classic, *7 Habits of Highly Effective People*, one habit is "Seek first to understand, then be understood." This is a great principle for mentors to adopt. If you really want to influence people, whether it is by imparting your wisdom or challenging their thinking, you need to understand them first.

Covey describes 5 levels of listening. At levels 1-4, we are hearing from our own perspective, focused on ourselves, and that means our understanding of the other is limited or non-existent.

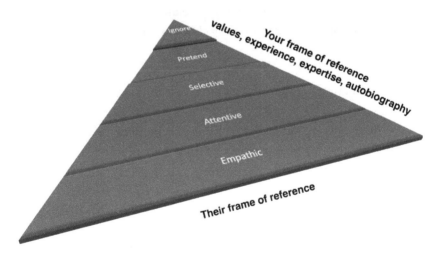

Levels of Listening. Covey, S (1989) 7 Habits of Highly Effective People. The Business Library.

LEVEL 1. Ignoring—whether deliberate or inadvertent, we've all experienced it. How does it make you feel? Those neurological responses described earlier trigger defensiveness, fight/flight/freeze. Maybe you never do this, but it can happen if you are preoccupied.

LEVEL 2. Pretend listening—you are going through the motions, nodding, saying, "OK," "I see," but you're distracted, not really paying attention. Or perhaps feel you should be polite, but you're really not interested.

LEVEL 3. Selective listening—paying attention to only parts of what is being said, easily slipping back into pretend listening, interrupting, or being impatient for people to get to the point.

LEVEL 4. Attentive listening—giving time and attention is good but, it can fall short of real understanding. Level 4 attentive listening often includes:

- Evaluating—judging based on *your* values, priorities and needs
- Advising—recommending from *your* point of view
- Probing—for information *you* think is important
- Interpreting—what's happening as *you* see it

As a mentor, listening well begins with setting a firm intention. What we aim for is level 5 empathic listening, because at levels 1-4 we're stuck in our own frame of reference, whereas in empathic listening we step into theirs.

LEVEL 5 EMPATHIC LISTENING—GENUINELY seeking to hear and understand the other person from their frame of reference.

"Truly understanding someone else's point of view does not come naturally. It's a learned skill that always requires effort."

Dan Bobinski (2016) The Price of Poor Listening. Management Issues.

Techniques for Better Listening

IF YOU WANT to be a better listener, develop these techniques:

SILENCE, don't interrupt, don't jump in with your own story, opinions, or advice. Let them speak.

FOCUS ON THEM, attend to what they are saying and what they are *not* saying. You want to understand what they mean and that doesn't always come out in the first words they say. Notice their non-verbal communication. Suspend your judgment and listen to their point of view. Try to pick up their values and priorities, needs and wants.

MINIMAL RESPONSE, you need to show them you are fully present and listening without interrupting their flow. So give positive non-verbal signs of listening. Keep your verbal responses short ("mm-hm", "I see", "tell me more") to encourage them to say more.

REFLECT, when it is your turn to speak, resist the urge to give advice! Instead, reflect back what they have said, emphasising their feelings. Don't parrot their words.Rather, paraphrase, summarise or restate using some of their words and some of your own.

ASK GOOD QUESTIONS. When you reflect, they will confirm or clarify their thoughts. Sometimes, that is all that they need. People often want to ventilate or express themselves. They're not seeking a solution from you! Even when they do need an answer, the opportunity to think out loud and be heard may be enough for them to come up with their own solution. If you do need to take the conversation further, do so with open questions, asked with respectful curiosity. And continue listening!

The activity below gives you a handy tool to remember the 5 techniques for better listening during a mentoring conversation.

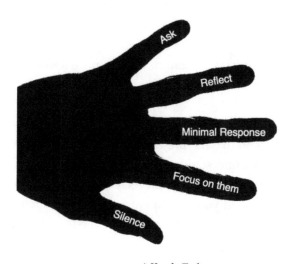

A Handy Tool

Activity: **A Handy Tool**

1. *Draw an outline of your hand on paper and label each finger as shown above.*
2. *Close your fingers with your thumb sticking out as if you were giving the thumbs up, but touch your thumb to your chin and as you do, say to yourself "silence". Do that again 3 times— touch your thumb to your chin and say "silence". This will be a reminder that the first step in really understanding what someone is saying is to keep quiet*

3. *With your thumb on your chin, it's quite easy and comfortable to lift your pointer finger to your lips, a further reminder to yourself to* **shhh.**

4. *Next, keeping your pointer finger extended, pivot your hand away from you toward an imaginary other person and say to yourself,* "*focus on them*". *Bring your hand back to the previous* "*shh*" *position and pivot back and forth 3 more times, repeating* "*focus on them*".

5. *Relax the pointer finger now and gently apply a small amount of pressure with your middle finger to the fleshy area beneath the thumb. What is the caption on your middle finger diagram? Repeat that now three times as you gently press that area with your middle finger.* "**Minimal response**, *minimal response, minimal response*".

6. *Now try to move your ring finger, just a little. Imagine you have a beautiful diamond ring, and it reminds you to* **reflect.** *Repeat to yourself* "*reflect, reflect, reflect*".

7. *Finally, raise your little finger. You've listened well and to go deeper, you need to* **ask.** *Remember, these are open questions, with respectful curiosity. Raise the little finger and repeat* "*ask, ask, ask*".

The Pareto Principle

Vilfredo Pareto (1848-1923) described a phenomenon now known as the 80:20 principle. Today, we usually apply it in project management, personal effectiveness, and business. Here, I'll show you how useful it is in mentoring.

Apparently, Pareto observed observed 20% of plants produced that 80% of peas in his garden. Studying income distribution, Pareto found that 20% of people owned 80% of the land. Industrial engineers and management thinkers have generalised Pareto's principle to a surprising number of areas. You may know, for example, that: 80% of business revenue comes from 20% of customers, 80% of results come from 20% of activities and people usually have 80% of the information needed to make a sound decision.

Applying Pareto's principle enables mentees to access their own wisdom *and* that of the mentor.

Excellent mentors spend 80% of their time listening and only 20% speaking! How can mentoring be so effective when the mentor speaks so little? Excellent mentors know that:

- Asking a question, then using empathic listening, encourages people to think for themselves. It allows people to reflect on their experience and gain insight;
- People come up with their own ideas, answers and options when given the opportunity to talk. Often all they need is a "sounding board"; and,
- When people feel heard, they feel respected and are more likely to listen and value the mentor's input when it is given.

The 80:20 principle also means is that mentees must speak80% of the time!

Mentees need to share their goals, interests, and concerns. Contrary to some people's expectations, being mentored is not sitting at the feet of the master, being told what to do.

Mentees also need to ask questions that draw out the mentor's expertise. Mentees can direct the conversation and get what they need by asking good questions.

The 80:20 ratio also applies to the content and process of a mentoring conversation.

- Content is *what* we speak about. The subject, topic, goals discussed.
- Process means *how* we discuss a topic. The tools, techniques, models applied to address an issue.

The mentee has 80% responsibility for the **content**. It is up to them to drive the agenda. The mentor's 20% of content allows them to introduce related topics, provide another perspective, share their experience or offer an opinion.

The onus is on the mentor for 80% of the **process**. Mentors facilitate decision-making, problem-solving or goal-setting and planning using appropriate tools, techniques and models.

The third application of Pareto's principle is this: some people think you meet with a mentor only when there is an issue or a problem to talk about.

A mentor *is* a useful sounding board and someone to turn to with difficulties, but that would be 20% or less of the purpose of mentoring. 80% of the time, mentoring will be about how the mentee is:

- Progressing toward goals
- Getting better outcomes
- Increasing job satisfaction and enjoyment, and
- Keeping aligned with their values and priorities.

Sometimes, a mentoring conversation is just about maintaining the relationship, so that later, when there *are* problems and issues to discuss, there is enough trust and respect to talk about them.

Both mentor and mentee need to listen well and ask good questions. When you do, it will amaze you how much tacit knowledge you can draw out and how inspiring it can be.

Activity: How Well do you Listen?

Below are some very common barriers to listening identified by Eastwood Atwater[1] in his book I Hear You. Give yourself a rating on each on a scale of:

0 = Never, 1 = Sometimes, 2 = Often, 3 = Always.

Only you will see the result so you can be as honest as your self-awareness allows.

When I listen, I find myself...

1. *Easily distracted*
2. *Faking attention*
3. *Reacting to emotional words*
4. *Interrupting frequently*
5. *Tuning out on uninteresting topics*
6. *Daydreaming if the speaker is slow*
7. *Jumping to conclusions*
8. *Finding fault with the message*
9. *Thinking of what I want to say*

How did you go? The highest score is 27, the lowest zero, but I think if any of us got that we're kidding ourselves. Obviously, the lower the score the better, but what I want you to do with this is to identify what you're worst at, because that gives you a goal to work towards improving.

14

THE ART OF QUESTIONING

Great mentors ask more questions than they answer. They are slow to give advice. They do not withhold their wisdom, but they will draw out their mentee's own first. The mantra for mentors could be:

Ask, before you tell;
listen, before you speak

I encourage you to use more questions in all your conversations because questions increase a person's self-awareness. There is evidence that suggests greater self-awareness leads to more confidence and creativity, sounder decisions, stronger relationships and more effective communication[1]. At work, self-awareness is associated with more satisfaction, more promotions, and more effective leadership.

Good Questions

The art of questioning is at the heart of mentoring. For mentors, good questions are those that cause the mentee to think deeply, explore, learn, plan, and experiment. There are lots of sample questions in the *Guide To Questioning* in the Tools and Guides section of this book. You've also seen the four fundamental questions in Chapter 6: A Mentoring Conversation.

As a mentor, you use questions to:

- Initiate exploration at the beginning of the relationship and when the mentee raises a new goal, topic or issue
- Facilitate learning when offering a new perspective or a different way of thinking about a situation
- Guide planning, once the mentee sets a goal and needs to figure out how to achieve it
- Support experimentation, encouraging the mentee to take action and try fresh approaches.

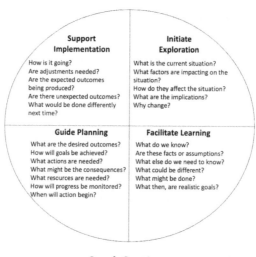

Sample Questions

INITIATING EXPLORATION

This involves reflecting on the current situation, a forthcoming change, or a problem. The mentor must judge whether the facilitative style (see Chapter 11: Communication Styles) raises the mentee's awareness enough to motivate the necessary learning and action planning. Sometimes, you can use the authoritative style. Bluntness doesn't mean brutality, but too much tact can prevent people from getting the message that *they* must change if they want their situation to change.

FACILITATING LEARNING

The assumption that people are intelligent and able to learn and solve problems for themselves is the basis of mentoring. Using the facilitative style, the mentor draws out the mentee's innate knowledge and insight. However, sometimes understanding dawns only when the mentor uses the authoritative style to provide information, facts or opinions that are outside the mentee's awareness.

GUIDING **Planning**

The mentee needs to set goals and plan action. The mentor may use the facilitative style, asking questions to prompt the mentee's thinking processes and elicit ideas. On the other hand, a significant benefit a mentor can offer is their own experience, their knowledge of what is likely to work and what isn't. So the authoritative style has its place, as the mentor makes recommendations and offers advice.

SUPPORTING **Experimentation**

This is the time when the mentee is implementing their plan. Using the facilitative style, the mentor offers encouragement and support. The mentor can also use the authoritative style, perhaps to coach or instruct, perhaps to give feedback or perhaps to confront their partner with unnoticed aspects of their actions.

Appreciative Inquiry

Appreciative Inquiry is based on Positive Psychology. It uses questions that assist people to appreciate positive aspects of themselves, their experience and their abilities and use that to explore aspirations and opportunities for their future.

It is Appreciative Inquiry that takes mentoring to a higher level, moving from problem-solving to positive change. Using positive psychology this way shifts from a deficit model (something's wrong) to a collaborative approach that identifies and amplifies potential. It offers an empowering context for mentoring where mentors guide mentees' progress by expanding options and providing the opportunity for self-discovery and positive action.

So, to increase the mentee's self-awareness, mentors use questions to explore their strengths, past successes, joy and energy, and values. For example:

- Describe your 3 greatest accomplishments to date.
- What brings you joy/most satisfaction/energises you?
- Who are your role models? What attributes do you admire and appreciate most?

There are more examples in *A Guide to Questioning* in the Tools and Guides section of this book.

The Art of Asking

"The mind is like an iceberg. It floats with one seventh its bulk above the water."

Sigmund Freud

A mentor's questions raise the mentee's self-awareness, bringing thoughts, feelings, ideas, aspirations from the deep to the surface.

It's important to help mentees recognise what they want, and check its alignment with their values by getting them to talk about why they want it. However, it's useful to have alternative ways to ask "why", because asking people *why* they want something, or *why* they do something or think something is problematic because it may:

- Trigger defensiveness/Justification
- Focus on fears, shortcomings and insecurities
- Entrench an existing mindset

Alternatives to "Why?"

- Instead of: Why do you want that? Try: What is it about that that's important for you?
- Instead of: Why do you feel that way? Try: What situations cause you to feel that way?
- Instead of: Why did you get a bad rating? Try: What might you do to get a better rating?

Three Ways to Ask

When you need to ask a lot of questions without it seeming like an interrogation, you need to listen well and without judgment, so that the other person feels safe to keep talking. Three simple techniques will assist you:

1. Cushions - Softening a Confronting Question

Combine these phrases with rapport-building, non-verbal communication to preface a confronting question. This reduces the chance of sounding like an interrogator.

- "Do you mind if I ask?"
- "I'm wondering..."

- "Would you like to tell me..."

2. Probing - Getting A Person To Talk More

- "Can you say a little more about..."
- "Would you expand on that idea?"
- "Perhaps you'd like to tell me..."

3. Summarising for Understanding

This gives you the opportunity to check that you've really understood what they've said. It also offers them the chance to further clarify - for themselves and for you - what they actually meant.

- "So, what you're saying is..."
- "What I'm hearing is..."
- "From your point of view..."

Activity: Good Questions

1. Look at the sample questions in A Guide to Questioning, in Mentoring Tools and Guides.
2. Write your own versions of some questions you could use in your own mentoring conversations.

15

GIVING AND RECEIVING FEEDBACK

Feedback may be the single most useful factor in self-development. Feedback lets us know whether our behaviour, knowledge, skills, or communication is achieving intended outcomes. It is information that tells that whether we need to adjust, apply more effort, or change our approach altogether.

Here's an example. A colleague was making a career transition. After years in one specialist field, she wanted to move into another. She knew she had transferable skills and expertise that were as relevant in the new field as the old one and prepared a resumé that sold her talents well. She got interviews for several senior positions but did not win the jobs. She was told she "came second" on several occasions. This was useful feedback. It told her she was not so far off-track that her goal was unlikely to be achieved, but provided insufficient information to make adjustments in her approach. Fortunately, she could eventually meet with a member of an interview panel and discuss her specific shortcomings. She learned that interviewers were put off because she used terminology from her old field instead of the industry jargon of the new one. Her choice of words was disqualifying her! It was easy for her to rectify that, and she got the next position for which she applied.

It takes courage, caring, and good communication to give or receive effective feedback. It is a step into the unknown that can unlock the hidden potential of unrecognised strengths and stumbling blocks.

The "Johari Window", developed by Joseph Luft and Harry Ingram,[1] provides a useful model for understanding the value of feedback.

In the diagram below, notice that self-disclosure and feedback increases open communication. You can build trust and respect and the skill to use both appropriately.

Feedback shrinks your blindspot and self-disclosure reduces what you normally keep hidden from view. This opens your potential personal and professional growth. The confidentiality of a mentoring conversation is an ideal space to explore this.

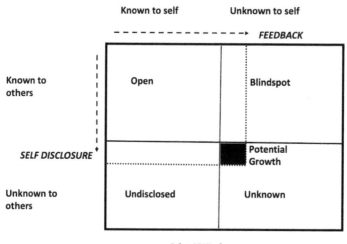

Johari Window

Some people talk about "constructive criticism". Others insist that criticism is never constructive, but it's clear that we need both positive and corrective feedback to stay on course.

Dr Matthew White[2] put it like this: positive feedback is like the wind in your sails. Corrective feedback is like a rudder to keep us on course.

It's important to get the ratio of positive and corrective feedback right. Even done well, feedback is not always going to be a positive experience, but we must find ways to try because decades of research have shown that we need positivity to outweigh negativity in our lives and in our workplaces if we are to flourish[3]. If the ratio is out of whack, relationships suffer, teams don't function well and people are less productive. There is a tipping point where people will languish or flourish. More positivity is better, up to a point, and less negativity is better, down to a point.

What if I told you there was a *simple* way to raise positivity *through feedback* that improves workplace performance on a range of measures?

Ochsner Health Care Services [4]in the US has 11,000 employees and educated all their leaders, physicians, nurses and support staff to implement what they call the 10/5 way and got these bottom-line building results.

- Increased unique patient visits
- Increased patient's likelihood to recommend the organisation
- Significantly improved medical practice provider scores

10/5 is a way of providing social support to work colleagues and patients. Research has linked social support to positive physical and emotional outcomes, employee engagement, and productivity. It's really simple:

If you walk within 10 feet of another person, you make eye contact and smile.
If you are within 5 feet, you say hello.

If you start 10/5 by yourself, or even with your team, it might feel silly and forced in the beginning, but building the habit has personal benefits and business ones. Eye contact, smiling and greeting are the most basic forms of feedback. It says: I see you. I respect you. I care.

3 Types of Feedback

There are three types of feedback you can use:

1. **Affirming:** positive feedback on behaviours you want people to keep doing
2. **Correcting:** behaviours you need them to do differently
3. **Reviewing:** when you collaborate, you find ways to do better

Typically, people do not get enough affirmation. That is, positive feedback.

So, in terms of feedback, we need to give much more affirming feedback than corrective feedback. Ken Blanchard's famously said *"catch them doing something right"*.[5] Yet most people do not get enough positive feedback. The trick to improving performance with feedback is getting the right balance of positive and corrective feedback.

I suggest you look for every opportunity to give affirming feedback. Behavioural psychology calls this positive reinforcement. It starts with eye contact and a smile, saying "thank you" letting people know you appreciate them. Nodding or making a brief comment lets a person know you're listening. Giving a genuine compliment and, of course, giving praise for good work, effort and achievement all reinforce behaviour and make it more likely to be repeated.

This not only increases positivity, it also builds trust and rapport and a culture where people feel respected and valued.

As well as reinforcing desirable behaviours, praise increases endorphin levels (the feel good hormone). It increases oxytocin (a bonding hormone), and reduces stress hormones. Sounds like a good recipe for better relationships to me!

Most of us can recall a time when we got valuable feedback. Sometimes it can create a turning point in our career or personal lives. Yet feedback can be difficult to get, hard to take, and even harder to give. A major difficulty is the level of discomfort experienced when people attempt to share what may be sensitive information.

Fear of Feedback

Sports people rely on measures of performance and strive for their personal best (PB), tracking it and using it as motivation to win and sometimes to cope with a loss. However, neuroscientists tell us that feedback about performance can feel threatening [6].

"Feedback about performance, in particular, tends to activate the brain's primary threat network, which produces a feeling akin to physical pain."

David Rock & Beth Jones

THIS MAY BE because of our experiences with traditional ratings-based appraisal, where ranking and labelling triggers the fight/flight/freeze reaction in the brain.

Because giving or receiving feedback can be painful and human beings naturally seek to avoid pain, we often react defensively. Defensiveness can take the form of denial, rejection or "counter-attack". Defensiveness can inhibit self-awareness. A key component of effective feedback, therefore, is to reduce the level of discomfort associated with feedback. Some general strategies include:

- Acknowledge the potential discomfort of the situation.
- Express thoughts and feelings appropriately.
- Be aware that language, voice, tone and non-verbal cues support or inhibit effectiveness.
- Focus on observable behaviour rather than inferred personality attributes. People may *do* things that seem stupid, but labelling a *person* stupid is counter productive.
- To provide motivation, discuss the likely consequences of continuing or changing actions.
- Maintain an outcome orientation. What result do they want? Why is it important to them?
- Keep a sense of proportion. Feedback is just information; it need not be a catastrophe.

When Giving Feedback:

- Avoid generalisations, vague or ambiguous descriptions. Offer specific examples: "you don't think strategically enough" is less helpful than "there are several major issues that you overlooked in your analysis."

- Acknowledge emotional responses, allow ventilation, but don't get sidetracked. Keep the communication goal-oriented. The purpose of feedback is to reflect on what happened in the past in order to improve actions in the future.
- Critique only actions within a person's control, but encourage them to take responsibility. For example, failure to complete a project on time because suppliers missed deadlines could be because of unforeseeable external factors, or it could result from poor project management.
- Develop improvement strategies. Ideally, you will elicit these during the discussion and provide suggestions when needed.
- Ensure that a plan of action is agreed and follow-up to review results. Acknowledge success and further adjustments needed.

When Receiving Feedback:

- Recognise the value of feedback - when you don't know, what you don't know you can't learn.
- Accept your emotions, but avoid overreacting and defer overt responses. Tears or tantrums in public do little for your professional image.
- Clarify information. Get specific instances. Ask why an action was problematic. Seek examples of alternative ways of handling the situation.
- Avoid defensive behaviour such as denial, rationalisation or blaming others. Excuses ease the pain, but they are also disempowering and can lead to feelings of victimisation and helplessness.

- Discuss strategies that will enable you to achieve desired
  outcomes. Think about the resources, support or coaching
  you may need and work out a plan to get it.
- Act on your plan, and provide feedback about the results
  to anyone considerate enough to have provided input.

As someone once said: "There's no such thing as mistakes—only
learning opportunities." Seeking feedback and handling it produc-
tively when you receive it will serve you well. You should evaluate the
feedback that others give by asking yourself three questions:

1. What is this person's intention? Why are they telling me
   this? If they have good intentions, like your wellbeing,
   professional development, better teamwork, outcomes,
   process improvement or other positive intent, it's worth
   hearing their input.
2. Is this feedback valid? It's probably valid from their point
   of view, but they may not have all the facts, or they may
   interpret the situation differently from you.
3. Does this person, the situation, or a better outcome matter
   to me? Should I care? I'm sure you know there are people
   out there that sound off for their own reasons that are
   nothing to do with you, they have no good intention, say
   ridiculous things and, as upsetting as they may be,
   actually they don't matter, unless you allow them to.

Assuming there's good intention, the feedback's valid, and it
matters, you then need to ensure the person giving it feels heard and
consider what you might do differently for a better result.

Past experience, strategies that have worked

Collaborative Review

When you receive feedback, treat it as a collaborative review. Envision what an ideal situation would look like, look at what's happening now and acknowledge the differences between the current reality and an ideal situation. Then, drawing from past experience, your strengths and strategies that might work, think about what is within your power to change. Finally, create an action plan to take the steps you are willing and able to do.

The response to affirming feedback, a compliment, praise is simply "thank you" or "I appreciate you saying that".

Activity: Practice Feedback

1. *Increase the frequency with wich you give positive feedback. Notice people's response.*
2. *Practice becoming more specific when you give feedback*
3. *Ask for feedback and respond positively.*

PART V

MENTORING TOOLS AND GUIDES

1. Quick Tips for Managing Your Mentoring Relationship
2. A Step-by-step Guide
3. A Mentoring Plan
4. Structure the Mentoring Meeting
5. Pre/post Meeting Checklist
6. A Guide to Roles and Responsibilities
7. The Mentoring Code
8. Activity: Expectations
9. Template: Mentoring Agreement
10. Activity: Dartboard
11. Activity: The Clock
12. Activity: Values Discovery
13. Strengths Discover Tools
14. Guide to Setting and Getting Goals
15. Simple Steps to Problem Solving and Decision-making
16. Ten Things to do With a Mentor
17. What to Talk About When There's Nothing to Talk About
18. Sample Questions

QUICK TIPS FOR MANAGING YOUR MENTORING RELATIONSHIP

1. Irregular or ad hoc contact often fails. A mentoring relationship depends on being organised. People who get the most out of mentoring **schedule regular contact**. It may be at the same time on a designated day, weekly, fortnightly or monthly, depending on the nature and duration of the mentoring agreement. The mentee should confirm arrangements 24 hours ahead of the appointment.
2. Time pressure is common. **Respect each other's time** by making mentoring a priority, confirming appointments, being on time and agreeing the frequency and duration of contact.
3. **Never cancel** an appointment, reschedule if it is absolutely necessary.
4. **Private space** and uninterrupted time are important for confidential conversation. However, a café provides a social setting that can be relaxing. Whatever environment you choose, the mentor and mentee need to feel safe to speak freely to each other.
5. Rapport means feeling comfortable in conversation. **Finding common ground**, shared interests or similarities

helps people feel at ease. A few minutes of "small talk" warms you up for more in-depth conversation.

6. A formal mentoring program usually provides guidelines. However, individuals need to **agree on some basic principles and logistics** for their relationship. Being politely upfront about expectations and limits is helpful to mentors and mentees.

7. Mentoring should have a purpose and, while specific goals may not be immediately obvious, **focussing on outcomes** gives the relationship direction.

8. **Be prepared.** If a mentee provides an agenda prior to each contact, mentors can be far more effective in responding to their needs. It doesn't have to be too formal, a simple list of discussion points, questions or issues is adequate.

9. A structured approach to the conversation will yield results. However, **flexibility** is important and good mentors respond to the mentee's needs.

10. Each mentoring contact should conclude with **two-way feedback**. It is important to acknowledge the value of the conversation and understand ways to improve it. I provide a process for this in the Relationship Review Templates.

A STEP-BY-STEP GUIDE

Step One: Your First Meeting

In the earliest stage of your mentoring relationship, aim to:

Get to know each other—by sharing something of your personal background and listening, so that each of you feels heard. Look for what you have in common and relish the interesting differences.

Become clear about expectations—whether or not you have explicit goals or outcomes planned, you want to have a good idea about why you are engaged in mentoring and what you hope for from each other. Use the activity *Expectations, A Guide to Roles and Responsibilities* and *The Mentoring Code* in this section of the book.

Plan—schedule regular meetings. Set one meeting aside after your third or fourth, to review the mentoring relationship.

Conclude by sharing feedback about your meeting. It may feel awkward, but you'll get more comfortable as it becomes a regular part of your mentoring conversation.

Step Two: Second Meeting

Prior to meeting again:

- Both review your agreed goals for mentoring

- Mentee confirms meeting time, duration and venue
- Both schedule uninterrupted time for the meeting
- Mentee drafts an agenda or discussion topics for the meeting and sends it to the mentor
- Both gather any necessary information or resources
- Both prepare questions to ask

At your second meeting, you may wish to flesh out A *Mentoring Plan* using the guide provided. It can be helpful to specify goals or outcomes. The overall purpose of mentoring is your main guide, goals evolve from that, so remain open and flexible.

Use the *Pre/Post Meeting Checklist* to use at each meeting to help you stay on track.

Step Three: Subsequent Meetings

Continue with regular contact.

Review the mentee's actions, outcomes, and achievements at each meeting.

Use the *Pre/Post Meeting Checklists* and/or the *Mentoring Plan* to track your progress.

Every three months have a discussion about the relationship. Talk about what is working well and what you might like to do differently.

Remember to:

- *Maintain* regular contact
- *Create* an appropriate environment
- *Establish* rapport and listen well
- *Observe* your ground rules
- *Be guided by* your mentoring purpose goals and plan
- *Prepare* for each conversation—mentee drafts an agenda;
- *Engage* in productive conversation
- *Ask for* and provide feedback on the process.

Step Four: Wind-up

Don't just let mentoring fizzle out. Failure to respond to your mentor/mentee is poor business etiquette and unacceptable in a mentoring program. If you are having difficulties, speak with the mentoring program coordinator. If you need to relinquish the mentoring relationship, the program coordinator will manage the exit strategy.

Conclude the mentoring relationship professionally. A celebration or acknowledgement of contributions and achievements ends mentoring appropriately.

A MENTORING PLAN

A written mentoring plan fleshes out the goals and describes how they are to be achieved. You can use as well as, or instead of, a written mentoring agreement. Consider your plan a work in progress, to be reviewed and amended, as necessary. Use the guide below:

1. Statement of Purpose

Discuss *why* the mentor and the mentee are entering the mentoring relationship. Describe the general aims.

2. Goals or Outcome

Describe what the mentee wants to achieve. The mentor will also have goals for how they want to proceed. As mentoring is a partnership, you will have joint goals for the relationship.

Specific goals may take some time to clarify. Don't get bogged down. Goals may become clearer, or change, as the relationship unfolds. Your statement of purpose will give you enough focus to get started.

3. Plan

Begin to plan *how* you will proceed:

- What specific actions will be taken by the mentee to achieve the goal?
- What specific actions/assistance will be available from the mentor?
- As well as the mentor, what other resources can the mentee access?

4. Time Plan

Discuss the frequency and duration of meetings and alternate forms of contact (phone, email, online, etc.). Schedule meeting /contact dates

STRUCTURE THE MENTORING MEETING

A simple format will ensure that your mentoring meeting is effective. These points apply whether you meet face-to-face, talk by phone or communicate via the Internet.

1. Rapport and Review

The first one or two meeting will dedicate more time to getting to know one another and finding common ground. Subsequent meetings still need to re-establish the connection. A mentoring conversation can be sociable as well as business-like.

2. The Agenda

Providing an agenda ahead of the meeting allows both parties to be prepared. Reviewing and agreeing, or amending it before you get too far into conversation, ensures you remain focussed.

3. The Mentoring Conversation

Use the format below as a guide and the *Sample Questions* in this section of the book to form your own questions suitable to the situation.

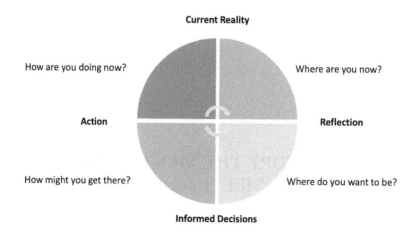

A Mentoring Conversation

4. Summarise Key Points

Summarising throughout the mentoring conversation maintains focus and ensures understanding. Towards the end of the time available for each meeting, the mentor can draw the conversation to its conclusion and move it into the next phase by listing the main points covered.

5. Next Steps

A productive mentoring relationship transforms ideas into action. The mentor asks the mentee to identify what they will do as a result of the conversation. The mentee commits to taking actions that you'll review together and discussed at the next meeting. An action plan creates energy and results.

6. Feedback

Feedback ensures that both parties are receiving and giving value in the relationship. Here are possible discussion questions:

1. What outcomes did we achieve in this meeting?
2. What did you value most, find useful or helpful?

3. What was difficult?
4. What would you rather do differently?
5. What insights did you gain?
6. What are you going to do as a result of this conversation?

PRE/POST MEETING CHECKLIST

Pre-Meeting Checklist

Have you:

- Reviewed your agreed goals for mentoring?
- Agreed on the agenda or discussion topics for this meeting?
- Confirmed meeting time, duration and venue?
- Scheduled uninterrupted time for the meeting?
- Gathered any necessary information or resources?
- Prepared questions you want to ask?

Post-Meeting Checklist

Have you:

- Summarised what what you discussed?
- Noted actions to be taken before next meeting?

- Obtained feedback about level of satisfaction with the mentoring process, communication style and progress toward outcomes?
- Agreed next meeting date?

A GUIDE TO ROLES AND RESPONSIBILITIES

The mentee can approach their mentor to discuss issues and ideas. The mentee may ask for feedback or advice or simply take the opportunity to express himself or herself, "get it off their chest". In speaking to their mentor, the mentee may find they gain greater clarity of a situation.

The mentor's questions or comments may cause the mentee to see another perspective, consider other options, and review their actions or plans. Whatever the matter discussed, it is the mentee who must make any decisions or take any actions required. The mentee is responsible for their own decisions and actions.

Responsibilities of a **mentor** include:

- Maintaining confidentiality of matters discussed
- Being accessible and providing an appropriate amount of time
- Listening empathically to the mentee
- Encouraging the mentee to see situations from more than one perspective and helping them to explore options
- Promoting responsible decision-making;

- Motivating and supporting the mentee in the achievement of their goals and referring them to various resources
- Ensuring a professional relationship, operating within the organisation's mentoring guidelines and policies
- Offering advice, when asked, without being directive and enabling the mentee to use problem-solving methods
- Acting as a role model, embodying the organisation's values and ethical standards; and
- Recognising when it is time to relinquish the role of mentor and doing so with good grace
- Other (add your own)

Responsibilities **mentee** include:

- Maintaining confidentiality of matters discussed
- Initiating contact and setting the agenda
- Candid discussion of issues
- Openness to considering various perspectives and options
- Gathering information from a variety of sources
- Making decisions and choices
- Taking action to achieve self-determined goals
- Ensuring a professional relationship, operating within the mentoring program guidelines and policies
- Acting within the program's values and ethical standards
- Concluding the relationship graciously
- Other (add your own)

THE MENTORING CODE

Both mentor and mentee will:

1. Maintain the confidentiality of the content their conversations, except in the case of disclosure of unlawful activities or threat of self-harm
2. Create an environment that enables both to focus on goals and professional development
3. Discuss each other's expectations of the relationship and how those expectations may be met
4. Recognise that the boundaries of mentoring are limited to professional and career-related goal achievement and that issues beyond this may require referral to another professional, such as a counsellor, therapist or specialist advisor
5. Appreciate that the mentor is not a professional consultant or intermediary and is not empowered to act on the mentee's behalf
6. Honour each other's time by managing accessibility and scheduling by mutual agreement

7. Fulfil their agreement to mentoring by staying in touch with their mentoring partner until the end of the program or an agreed relinquishment of the relationship

8. Understand that mentoring relationships exemplify dignity, autonomy and personal responsibility

9. Regularly review and provide feedback about their mentoring experience to each other

10. Ensure that they act with integrity and in such a way as to cause no harm to each other

11. Respect diversity and equity

12. Avoid exploitation of the relationship

13. Conduct themselves professionally and in a manner that reflects positively on the profession, the organisation and the mentoring program

14. Conclude the relationship respectfully when it ceases to be useful

ACTIVITY: EXPECTATIONS

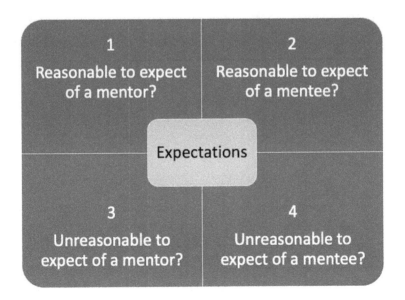

1. What is reasonable to expect of your mentor?
2. What is reasonable to expect of your mentee?

3. What is unreasonable to expect of your mentor?
4. What is unreasonable to expect of your mentee?

TEMPLATE MENTORING AGREEMENT

We commit to:

1. Regular Contact

- **Method(s):** Can we get together in real-time, face-to-face, phone, or online (FaceTime/Skype/Zoom etc.) Or, by email or online platform?
- **Term:** Over what period of time do we intend the mentoring to take place?
- **Frequency:** How often will we meet or be in touch?
- **Duration:** How long will we meet for each time?)

2. Professional Courtesy

Specific expectations (e.g. confirming appointments, preparing and agenda, being on time, etc.)

3. Ground Rules

What we will and won't do (e.g. maintain confidentiality)

4. Scope and Boundaries

Topics we will/will not discuss:

Signed (Mentor):

Signed (Mentee):

Date

ACTIVITY: DARTBOARD

This approach takes into account *all* the important areas of your life and allows you to make balance and integrity features of how you live.

The **Dartboard** exercise is powerful. Take your time, work in pencil and begin to design the next year of your life.

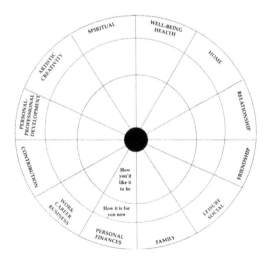

1. Take a large (A3) piece of paper. Draw the largest circle you can fit on it. Now draw a second and third concentric circle within the first.
2. Divide the circle into about 12 segments by drawing straight lines and put a "bull's eye" in the centre so the diagram resembles a dartboard.
3. Brainstorm a list of the important areas of your life for which you need goals e.g. relationship, family, career, health, money, spirituality, professional development, social contribution, fun, friends, hobbies, home, sport etc. Use these to label each segment in the outer ring.
4. Working on one segment of the dartboard, one important area at a time, write in the next ring, a brief description of how that aspect of your life is now.
5. When you have completed how it is now, move to the inner circle of each segment and describe, ideally, how you would like that part of your life to be.
6. Wherever you have a difference between how it is and how you'd like it to be, you have the scope to set goals. These are not yet goals, but they are the foundation of your goal setting.
7. In the bull's eye, write the letter "I" to remind you that *you* are at the centre of your circle of influence. *You* have the most control over your own thoughts, feelings, words, and deeds. The "I" also stands for integrity, being true to your highest values and drawing together all the important parts of your life, rather than allowing them to pull you in different directions.

ACTIVITY: THE CLOCK

This is a practical way of gaining insight and motivation as a basis for goal setting.

1. Take a sheet of paper and draw a large circle. Create an analog clock face by writing "12", "3", "6" and "9" in the appropriate spots. Draw the "big hand" of your clock pointing to 12. Above the "12" put zero.
2. Consider the next question quickly—your intuition will provide an answer and you can always change your mind later. Here is the question: To what age do you expect to live? Write this number to the left of the zero.
3. Now, using the zero and the number you just wrote as your life expectancy, draw the "little hand" on the clock face according to your present age. For example, if you said you'd live to 100 and you are now 50, the little hand points to 6 o'clock.
4. You have divided your circle into two parts, past and future. Your next task is to list, on the right side of the clock, your significant achievements to date. Record accomplishments of which you are proud, things you're

glad you've done, experiences you've had and times you have been exactly who you want to be. Don't get hung up on words like "achievement" or "accomplishment". Whatever matters to you, matters.

5. Next, list on the left the things you'd not want to leave undone when you go. Whether it's learning to sing, travel, reconciling old differences, reuniting with loved ones, material accoutrements, providing for others, or simply satisfying your self. Write from the heart, describe your desires, list what matters to you.

6. You may wish to sort this list into ideas for the next five years, the five after that and the five after that. You will also break your first five years into lists for each year once you have decided which of these to make goals for action and which to leave on a wish list.

7. Most people like to spend the last part of life relaxing, smelling the roses or otherwise enjoying the fruits of life's labour. If you wish, draw another line, at the point of your choice, to indicate your age of retirement on the clock. You can now calculate the number of years left to achieve the financial security you'll need then. You also have a time frame for travel plans or experiences for which youth and strength are helpful. Identify other important points on the clock. If you have children, at what age will they no longer be dependent? Are there other age-related goals or changes?

ACTIVITY: VALUES DISCOVERY WORKSHEET

Rating Scale 1 = Very important, 2 = Moderately important, 3 = Not important

Achievement: desired outcomes resulting from persistent endeavour

1 2 3

Aesthetics: appreciation and enjoyment of beauty and artistic experiences

1 2 3

Altruism: active concern for the needs and values of others

1 2 3

Ancestry: those who came before us; our line of descent

1 2 3

Autonomy: the drive to be an independent, self-determining individual

1 2 3

Community: people who care about something and pursue it together

   1 2 3

Competency/Skill: competence in performing given tasks

   1 2 3

Control/Influence: authority or influence over others

   1 2 3

Creativity: the ability to transcend traditional ideas, rules, patterns, relationships, or the like to create meaningful new ideas, forms, methods and interpretations

   1 2 3

Dignity: demonstrate behaviour and stature that earn the respect of self and others

   1 2 3

Emotional Well-being: inner peace, abiding confidence, freedom from anxieties, tranquility

   1 2 3

Family: person(s) with whom you have an emotional and/or biological bond

   1 2 3

Harmony: unity in relationships; the absence of conflict and strife between associates

   1 2 3

Health: soundness of body, mind and spirit

   1 2 3

Honesty: truth, openness, fairness, integrity

1 2 3

Honour: recognition given to one who has distinguished him/herself from peers by living a life of superior standing
1 2 3

Humility: the ability to be honest with yourself, meek, teachable, open to change
1 2 3

Justice: behaviour that conforms to what is right, fair and reasonable
1 2 3

Knowledge: fact and lessons learned, understanding/awareness of principles that organise and explain
1 2 3

Love: unselfish devotion that freely accepts another person
1 2 3

Loyalty: maintained allegiance to a person, group, institution or idea
1 2 3

Passion: the "fire within" that brings rewards beyond any monetary gain or satisfaction from your hard work
1 2 3

Personal Growth: Lifelong learning, continuous improvement, wisdom
1 2 3

Physical Appearance: concern for the attractiveness of one's own body
1 2 3

Pleasure: enjoyment and gratification delivered from that which is to one's liking

1 2 3

Recognition: favourable attention and acknowledgement from others that makes one feel significant

1 2 3

Relationships: being surrounded by people who like you and care about you

1 2 3

Spirituality/Religion: a set of beliefs concerning the cause, nature, and purpose of the universe. Communion with, and activity in a relationship with a higher power.

1 2 3

Wealth: an abundance of valued material possessions and resources. Economic prosperity.

1 2 3

Now highlight your top 7 from the above list. Then number your top 3 in priority order.

Use this information to review your "Dartboard" and "Clock". Choose an area in which to set a goal.

STRENGTHS DISCOVERY TOOLS

Journal

I recommend a reflective journal. It will take some time, but can be extremely rewarding to write introspectively putting your thoughts and feelings on paper. Here are some thought-starter questions you could reflect on:

1. What do you look forward to doing most at work?
2. Which activities do you complete quickly and easily?
3. What do you enjoy doing most outside of work?
4. What did you enjoy doing most in previous roles?
5. What do other people say you do best?
6. What are you known for?
7. What is your dream job? Why?
8. After living expenses, what do you spend your money on?
9. What did you love as a child?
10. What would friends and co-workers say were your talents?

These questions are great for a mentor to discuss with a mentee, but probably require some reflective thinking time for the mentee first.

Then, this information can be used to pick up clues to talents and strengths. In terms of personality, do the answers reveal more of a doer, persuader, people-person or someone who loves information?

Thirty-Day Challenge

1. Every day, at least once a day, stop and reflect: what did I do well?
2. Write it down - especially if you enjoyed it, especially if you felt strong when you did it!
3. At the end of thirty days, share with your mentoring partner. Look for patterns and evidence of your talent themes and strengths.

Online Strengths Assessment

The instrument I recommend to discover talents and strengths and the one I use in coaching, mentoring programs and workshops is the CliftonStrengths Assessment. You can purchase this and do it online. It comes with detailed reports and a great deal of helpful information about using your results. Or you can buy a hard copy book which comes with a code for the online instrument, here:

www.gallupstrengthscentre.com

GUIDE TO SETTING AND GETTING GOALS

Goal setting is pretty easy, it's *getting* the goal that's the challenge. So many things can get in the way!

This guide will help you set *and get* goals.

Before you go any further read the Chapter 8 *On Goals*. Then do these activities, if you've not already done so:

1. The Dartboard
2. The Clock
3. Values Discovery

Now you're ready to use the research into what works and what doesn't for setting and getting goals as you map out a detailed plan to achieve the goal you choose.

Exercises like The Dartboard and The Clock can be a wake-up call! Neither produces goals, but they highlight desires you can add to your wish list. You must consciously choose those you desire *enough* to make goals.

Both these activities help you think about priorities. The Values

Discovery Worksheet takes this a step further and helps you identify what you care most about.

Goal Map

To achieve any important goal, you need an action plan. The Goal Map activity becomes an at-a-glance road map of your goal. It will help keep you motivated and on track. It's a visual reminder of continuous, consistent progress.

Take a large sheet of paper, A3 is good, and draw the diagram above.

Step One: Aim

Once you have completed the activities mentioned above, select an aim you're going to work on. You might choose an area from your dartboard where there is a difference between how it is and how you'd like it to be. Or perhaps, something that would make a difference to your life/work balance. Choose something real for you. An aim is something you'd like to change or achieve. It can be quite broad and general for now—we'll get more specific a little further on in this process. For now, simply outline what you want to accomplish. Here are some examples:

- Better work-life balance
- A promotion
- Improved financial situation

Write your aim now:

Map "Why"

Motivation is very high when you first set a goal, but things happen along the way. If the "why" of your goal is not compelling enough, there will not be enough intrinsic motivation or desire to carry you through what happens along the way. Find a better "why" or find a better goal!

It helps if you can think out loud in a conversation with a mentor or buddy, but for now, think about:

- How will achieving this benefit you, others and/or a cause that you believe in?
- What would happen if you did not make the effort (what are potential consequences)? List the reasons these consequences are important to you.
- How this goal aligns with your values
- Is there an underlying issue, aim or purpose, a goal behind the goal?
- Ultimately, what is the goal really about (your intention)?

Summarise your answers on your goal map:

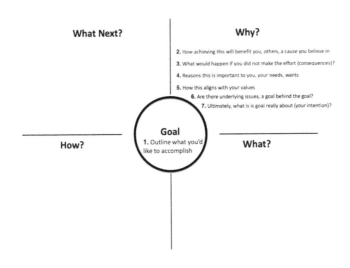

At this point, some people realise they have set the wrong goal. Reflect and re-assess. Do you need to amend, modify, or change your goal? Or has this confirmed your goal and that you are ready to commit to it? If so, you're ready to get specific.

Map What?

Answer these questions:

- What specifically is the outcome you are after?
- What evidence will tell you that you've succeeded (how will you know)?
- What is your timeframe? When will you start? Realistically, how long will it take?
- What will you monitor to track your progress over time?
- What resources do you need to accomplish this goal (time, money, information, skills, knowledge, support)?

Summarise your answers on your goal map:

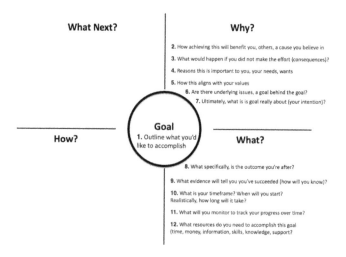

Map "How"

Your Goal Map has helped you identify **why** this goal is important to you. It has described in detail **what** you want to achieve and what will indicate progress as well as success. Now it's time to look at exactly how you'll go about it.

List the steps on the way to your goal:

List obstacles, setbacks and challenges that might get in the way of achieving your goal:

List ways you'll get over or around these obstacles:

List some habits that might hold back the change you want:

List some behaviours that would be more useful than the habits above:

Consider:

- What talents and strengths will help you?
- What stands in the way (barriers, obstacles)?
- How have you overcome similar challenges?
- What do you need to do? Are there steps and stages?
- What might get in the way of these actions (beliefs/habits)?
- How will you change unhelpful beliefs or habits?
- How willing are you to take these actions (level of commitment)?
- How will you keep yourself accountable (buddy/mentor/team)?

Summarise your responses on your Goal Map:

What Next?

Why?

2. How achieving this will benefit you, others, a cause you believe in

3. What would happen if you did not make the effort (consequences)?

4. Reasons this is important to you, your needs, wants

5. How this aligns with your values

6. Are there underlying issues, a goal behind the goal?

7. Ultimately, what is is goal really about (your intention)?

Goal
1. Outline what you'd like to accomplish

How?

20. How will you keep yourself accountable (buddy/mentor/team)?

19. How willing are you to take these action s (commitment)?

18. how will you change unhelpful beliefs or habits?

17. What might get in the way of these actions (beliefs/habits)?

16. What do you need to do? Are there steps and stages?

15. How have you overcome similar challenges?

14. What stands in the way, (barriers, obstacles)?

13. What talents and strengths will help you?

What?

8. What specifically, is the outcome you're after?

9. What evidence will tell you you've succeeded (how will you know)?

10. What is your timeframe? When will you start? Realistically, how long will it take?

11. What will you monitor to track your progress over time?

12. What resources do you need to accomplish this goal (time, money, information, skills, knowledge, support?

Additional Activity: Mental Contrasting

Heidi Grant Halvorsen[1] recommends the technique of mental contrasting to get a clear picture, a feeling of success, compare where you want to be with where you are now and realise what might get in the way.

Do this now:

Close your eyes and imagine how you will feel, the emotions you will experience, achieving your goal. Picture it vividly and in detail. What will you see, hear, the tangible evidence of accomplishing your goal? Then think about what's between you and your goal, the obstacles and effort required. Keep comparing where you are and where you want to be, so the need for change becomes compelling.

Hints and Tips

- Remember to reach out to people who can help. Jot some names down now:
- Decide how often you'll check progress and set reminders on your calendar.

Changing Habits That Don't Serve You

Michael Bungay-Stanier[2] in his YouTube video *Building Rock Solid Habits* describes using ABC as a formula for changing habits that don't serve you (see Chapter 8 On Goals).

A   B   C

Trigger   Old Habit   New Habit

The B stands for the old habit, behaviour that you want to change. *Briefly describe that here:*

Before B comes A, something that activates the behaviour. When does it happen? What sets you off? What circumstances trigger it? *Outline the context here:*

C is a new habit, something you will do instead. It needs to be quick (60 seconds or less) and easy. *Write that now:*

Create some "If... Then" rules to support new habits:

e.g. If it is 6 am on a week-day, then I'm going for a walk.

Complete Your Goal Map
The "What Next" quadrant incorporates the ideas described in Chapter 8 On Goals into your at-a-glance plan.

- Set rules (if-then) reminders
- Build your will-power muscle
- Track how far you've come AND what's left
- Focus on getting better, not being good (growth mindset)
- Notice what's changing, persist/adjust
- Recognise and reward yourself

Summarise your actions on your Goal Map:

Keep Your Goal Front of Mind

If you've done the hard yards of thinking this goal through and mapping it out, you need a way to keep it front of mind. Choose a single word that represents the goal. Something that will be a reminder. Put it on a post it note where you can see it. Make it a screen-saver on your phone. Write it in your diary. Do what ever works for you to see this word every day.

Write your word for this goal now:

SIMPLE STEPS TO PROBLEM SOLVING AND DECISION-MAKING

The mentor's objective is to enable the mentee to make an informed decision. Classic decision-making and problem-solving models incorporate the following five steps.

1. Analyse The Situation

Discuss the issue from the mentee's perspective. Identify facts and acknowledge feelings. Explore alternative viewpoints and gather more information if need be.

2. Set Objectives

Compare the current reality to the ideal situation. The mentee describes the way they'd like it to be. The conversation describes a desirable and realistic outcome.

3. Generate Alternative Strategies

Avoid fixating on a solution too quickly. Mentoring allows you to use processes like brainstorming options. Developing several options increases possibilities and produces better choices.

4. Evaluate Options

Talking about the pros and cons of each alternative allows the mentee to explore the options fully and think about the effort, benefits and other consequences of any actions.

5. Decide

The mentee selects the best option for himself or herself.

TEN THINGS TO DO WITH A MENTOR

Regular conversations that are useful and productive help you maintain a mentoring relationship. Yet people may struggle to come up with something to talk about with their mentor, especially when they don't have a particular problem or goal, or feel they don't need specific guidance. As a result, there's a danger mentoring may fizzle out.

Here are ten ways to keep mentoring vibrant and alive by injecting challenge and change.

1. **Book club**—both read a chapter of a relevant book each week/month and discuss how it applies in your situation and what you could action.
2. **Psychometrics**—use the results of an instrument such as Myers-Brigg Type Indicator, Clifton Strengths Assessment, Life Styles Instrument, DISC or any sort of 360° feedback as a basis for development.
3. **My life as a movie**—pick (or imagine) a movie that represents your life. Which character are you? How do the events in the movie reflect your life/career?

4. **Glasshouse**—visit the mentor in their workplace. Have them explain their job/business and ask lots of questions.
5. **Shadow**—accompany the mentor to meetings or in their daily work, as a silent observer. Then ask questions and discuss what you learned.
6. **Play journalist**—Prepare a list of questions about the mentor's career or experience and interview them.
7. **Research** and reflect—do some fact-finding about a relevant topic. Discuss what you discovered and how you might use it.
8. **Rehearse**—practice a conversation that you need to have with your manager or a colleague, or a job interview. Get feedback and coaching from your mentor to produce the outcomes you want.
9. **Artwork**—draw a picture/make a collage or vision board to represent where you see yourself going or what's important to you.
10. **Write your obituary or eulogy**—this sounds a bit dark, but if you've ever read an obituary or heard a good eulogy, you know it can be a celebration of all that was positive in one person's life. So make this about what you'd like to be remembered for. Perhaps you triumphed over adversity. Maybe you were accomplished in many areas. Use your imagination and make it as positive as possible.

WHAT TO TALK ABOUT WHEN THERE'S NOTHING TO TALK ABOUT

In the time-poor environment that we have created, mentees are more concerned than ever about wasting their mentor's time. Mentees are often hesitant to contact their mentor or schedule meetings when they have no burning issue to discuss. This is a mistake.

No Problem

Mentoring conversations are not just about solving problems or making decisions. They are about the availability of a person with whom to have a conversation that provokes creative and critical thinking. A key benefit of mentoring is the relationship itself. It needs to be established and well maintained so that the mentee can share problems or important decisions confidently when they arise.

Conversations about what is going well are extremely useful, too. Celebrating success is not simply a feel-good exercise. The purpose of mentoring is to create and capture insight, and then use it. Reviewing positive outcomes and satisfaction will reveal and reinforce the constructive behaviours that led to success and clarify personal values and priorities. By listening and questioning, a mentor can facilitate a much greater awareness of positive actions that will enhance the mentee's life.

Long-term Goals

People often use mentoring to identify career direction and work towards it. They rarely achieve these goals overnight, rather as a result of specific actions over time. So naturally, there will be pauses in between. In a mentoring program over a finite period, the early momentum can come to a halt after initial actions. Some mentoring relationships can survive long gaps between contacts, but most won't. So it is useful to have a "default agenda" to produce constructive conversation. This could be as simple as reviewing the week/fortnight/month's highlights and low points and accomplishments. The mentor may ask a series of questions that prompt reflection and learning, such as "what's working well for you, right now?" and "what could you improve?" A new, short-term goal and actions, or at least awareness and focus, often result.

Personal Development

No matter what qualifications, age, or career stage you have achieved, ongoing personal development is a must. Even where a mentee has an individual development plan negotiated with a manager and linked to performance appraisal, taking personal responsibility is essential. It is easy to let the demands of day-to-day work and a hectic lifestyle get in the way of personal aspirations and growth as a human being. If we lose sight of what is truly important, if we have no sense of purpose, life can become a meaningless round of chores, interspersed with moments of instant gratification. Mentoring conversations are all about discovering meaning and purpose–for mentors as well as mentees. The mentor might share his or her own life-lessons and insights that led to personal development. This can be immensely valuable to both parties.

We should not underestimate the social support offered by relationships in the too-busy life so many of us lead. When you don't have time, or have nothing to talk about, it may be *exactly* the time to have a mentoring conversation! Investing time and really communicating with another human being, taking time out to pause and reflect, or simply stopping to smell the roses (or the coffee) is never a waste of time!

SAMPLE QUESTIONS

In this section you'll find sample questions you can adapt for your mentoring conversations.

To initiate exploration, ask:

- What factors are affecting the situation?
- How do they affect the situation?
- What are the implications?
- Why change?

To facilitate learning, ask:

- What do we know?
- Are these facts or assumptions?
- What else do we need to know?
- What could be different?
- What, then, are realistic goals?

To guide planning, ask:

- What are the desired outcomes?
- How might you achieve these goals?
- What actions would you need to take?
- What might be the consequences of the actions contemplated?
- How will it be done?
- What resources would you need?
- How will you monitor progress?
- When will action begin?

To support experimentation, ask:

- How is it going?
- Are adjustments needed?
- Are the expected outcomes being produced?
- Are there unexpected outcomes?
- What would you do differently next time?

Questions to Help People SOAR

Strengths

- What do you do really well?
- What are your greatest achievements so far?
- What has helped you accomplish this?
- What are you most proud of?
- What attributes enabled you to do that?
- What three adjectives to describe you, at your best?
- What do you regard as your greatest strength?
- What do you see as your biggest asset?
- What challenges have you overcome?
- How did you do that?
- What do others compliment you on?

Opportunities

- In what situations do you excel?
- How does what you do help others/the organisation?
- What could you change to get better outcomes?
- What motivates you?
- What do you want to learn or develop?
- Where do you see that you have a contribution to make?
- What help and support can you give/get from others?
- Who is the most motivated person you know? What strategies do they use to keep motivated?
- What are your challenges or obstacles and how can you reframe them as opportunities?
- How can you draw on your strengths and abilities?

Aspirations

- Where do you want to be in a year's time?
- What is important to you?
- What are you aiming for?
- Who are your role models?
- What are your values?
- What do you want to be remembered for?
- What roles attract you?
- Are there things you haven't experienced yet that you want to?
- What's your vision for yourself?
- Look into the distant future; see yourself as happy, successful and fulfilled. Describe the scenario.

Results

- What outcomes do you intend to achieve?
- What would success look like for you?

- How will you know that you have achieved your goal?
- How will you measure the results?
- What are the reasons you want to achieve this goal? What will it do for you? What will you get?
- What do you want to be known for?
- What is the legacy you want to leave?
- What does life-balance mean to you?
- If you were truly satisfied, describe how it would be?

Questions to Clarify Values

- Who are your heroes or role models?
- What qualities do you most admire in them?
- What fires you up?
- What's most important to you?
- How would you spend your time if you didn't need to work?
- Describe a dream day?
- What do you do outside of work?

Questions to Use In a Career Discussion

- What is most important to you in your life and work?
- How happy are you with your work-life balance?
- Which are the skills you are best at and enjoy using most?
- How satisfactory is your current level of performance?
- Which areas of your performance would you like to improve?
- What are you passionate about?
- What potential constraints must you consider when planning your career?

Questions for Skills Development Discussion
This conversation compares the current actual situation to an ideal future scenario. Then identifies what needs to change.

- What changes are you likely to need to deal with in the near future?
- What results would you like to achieve that you are not achieving now?
- What new skills do you want to develop?
- What skills do you want to improve?
- Which areas of your performance need to improve?
- What knowledge, information or qualification do you need to gain in the near future?
- In terms of skills, how might you close the gap between where you are and where you want to be?

Open Questions

Open questions begin with who, what, where, how, or when. These help elicit information. In contrast, closed questions usually get a yes or no response.

Question Generalisations

You can challenge sweeping generalisations that are usually negative and limiting, such as "this always happens to me", "everybody knows…".

Prompt a rethink by asking:

"Always?"

"Everybody?"

Clarifying Questions

Take the fuzziness out of words and statements that are broad, vague, and open to interpretation:

"What specifically, do you mean by…"

"Which particular…"

"How, specifically..."

Diagnostic Questions

We aim these at finding the root of a problem, separating symptoms from causes, probing issues and prompting reflection on experience. Examples include:

"Why do you think they responded that way?"

"What other factors are contributing to the situation?"

Information Seeking Questions

There is often a need to gather facts and perceptions in a mentoring conversation. It is also important not to make assumptions and not to move into problem solving until you're sure you have a real understanding of the situation. Questions might include:

"How did you respond to that?"

"What did you do about this?"

"What options have you considered?"

Challenge Questions

Just remember to keep your non-verbal communication supportive when using challenge questions. Adopt an attitude of curiosity. Examples of challenge questions are:

"What are your reasons for saying that?"

"What has led you to that conclusion?"

"Do you think other people would see it that way?"

Action Questions

Mentoring is not just about talking; it is about enabling the mentee to make informed decisions and act on them. Prompt action planning by asking:

"What could you do to improve the situation?"

"How might you go about achieving that?"

"What specifically, do you plan to do?"

Priority & Sequence Questions

People sometimes do not achieve their goals and plans because they feel overwhelmed or don't know where to start. Sorting out what they can do and in what order can clarify thinking and break the task into manageable chunks.

"What will you do first?"

"What is the next step?"

"Is there a logical order in which to proceed?"

Prediction Questions

Remaining non-directive can be a challenge. Yet sometimes, you will see potential pitfalls in someone else's plan. In big decisions, consideration of possible consequences is essential. Therefore, prediction questions are good risk management:

"What are the likely consequences of this?"

"Are there other possible repercussions?"

"If you do nothing, what will happen?"

Hypothetical Questions

Thinking and talking through scenarios allows practice in a safe environment and can lead to a rehearsal or role-play of a planned event to build skills.

"What would you do if..."

"How would you handle..."

Extension Questions

Critical thinking skills are an asset that increases one's ability to learn and grow. Develop these skills by asking such questions as:

"What are the implications of..."

"What insights have you gained as a result?"

"What have you learned from this incident?"

Learning Questions

Current and past experience provides important learning opportunities as long as we take time to reflect and draw useful conclusions. Questions that prompt this include:

"What could you do differently next time?"

"How is this situation like others you have dealt with?"

Feeling Questions

The questions described so far promote sound, logical, and rational decision-making. However, humans are driven by emotions. They will not enact a logical decision unless it is inspired by emotion. Motivation is emotion, the energy that moves us toward or away from an outcome. Mentoring allows a healthy balance of decisions using the head and the heart. Ask:

"How do you feel about that?"

"How is that sitting with you?"

"What is your heart telling you?"

EVALUATE YOUR MENTORING RELATIONSHIP

If you are in a structured mentoring program, there will be an evaluation process. If not, use these discussion starters to share feedback.

Activity: Relationship Review

1. What did you each get out of the mentoring experience?
2. To what degree was good rapport established?
3. Were the mentee's needs addressed?
4. Did you achieve the goals nominated at the outset of the mentoring?
5. Were meetings of appropriate duration and frequency?
6. Has the mentee's ability to produce and sustain self-development improved as a result of mentoring?
7. How satisfied is the mentee with counsel and advice provided?
8. Was constructive and encouraging feedback provided when needed?
9. Was the mentee encouraged to accept responsibility for his or her own development?

10. What demonstrable outcomes can you attribute to the mentoring relationship?
11. Did the relationship end at the appropriate time and in an appropriate manner?
12. Was the level of support provided by the organisation adequate?

WHERE TO FROM HERE?

As your mentoring draws to a close, does it just end or is it a new beginning?

It's said:

"People come into your life for a reason, a season or a lifetime and when you know which one it is, you will know what to do for each person."

As a formal mentoring program ends, you and your mentoring partner get to decide whether the reason for the mentoring has been fulfilled and the season of your relationship is over, or whether to continue informally and indefinitely.

Mentoring relationships evolve. For some, mentoring morphs into friendship—though it's fine if it doesn't—some highly successful mentoring is kept strictly professional. Usually, there has been growth and change for both parties.

Sometimes, the respect each has for the other leads to reciprocal mentoring. Others are happy to remain in contact as professional colleagues. And for some, the conclusion of the program signals the end of the relationship.

Before you decide, consider the purpose of mentoring. Mentoring enables you to make informed decisions and create the future you want.

There are three key needs that mentoring addresses:

1. Lifelong learning has never been more important and mentoring enables both the mentee and the mentor to develop and grow;
2. It's more and more evident that our wellbeing depends on interaction with others and the support we give and get in relationships, such as mentoring; and,
3. Another perspective brings wisdom to decision-making. Difference, diversity and even discordant ideas make us smarter if we can hear and explore alternate views.

I recommend you take a little time to review what you have achieved through your mentoring relationship. Take stock of where you are now so that you can choose where to from here.

If you're part of a mentoring program, there may be a group session as a finale, where you may workshop ideas about the future with your peers. There are some review questions below so you can prepare for that, discuss with your mentoring partner or simply reflect and consider for yourself.

1. Why did you opt for mentoring?
2. Did you get what you were hoping for?
3. What have been the results for you?
4. What was your biggest challenge?
5. What did you value most about the mentoring?

It's likely that your mentoring conversations offered opportunities for goal setting, personal strategic planning, exploration of your values, career planning, and discovery of your strengths. It's good to do some activities in this book, such as Dartboard and The Clock, regularly to take stock of where you are before making future plans. These activities will enable you to set your next goals for self-development, career satisfaction, and how you want to live life. Just because the mentoring finishes doesn't mean you stop planning and achieving what you want!

Make self-development a priority—they say you are green and growing or ripe and rotting! In the rapidly changing world we live in, it's never been more important to keep honing skills, learning new things and expanding your capabilities. Schedule time each week to stay up to date, or better still, cutting edge, in your own field and dabble in other areas of interest too.

Be proactive in safeguarding your wellbeing. Exercise your body and your mind, but remember that interaction with others, and the support we give and get in relationships are vital to our health and wellbeing. There is a reason that the safety demonstrations on airplanes instruct you to fit your own mask first, before helping others. Taking care of yourself is especially important when you have work, family or community commitments that ask a lot of you.

Who you hang out with is important. You need variety and balance in your life. Seek and try to understand people who have a different perspective from you. Talk to people from different walks of life, with different interests and hobbies. Really listen to them. Do different things. It's not just travel that broadens the mind. Sport, art, and leisure activities offer another way of looking at the world. Open your mind to new possibilities, consider alternatives and gather information so that you make informed decisions about important matters.

There is one way you can do all of this for yourself and for others, too. You can probably guess what it is. As you're deciding "where to from here" consider mentoring someone else. If someone has mentored you this time, mentoring someone else is a way to "pay it forward". If you have been the mentor, hopefully, you've gained so much that you are willing to do it again. There are many opportunities for informal mentoring conversations or mentoring moments within or outside your organisation. You might volunteer in a formal program within your organisation, out in the community, or perhaps a university alumni program, and if you are a manager, you ought to mentor and coach your subordinates. Manager as mentor is a different type of relationship from the off-line mentoring that is the feature of most organisational programs and there are some articles on my website in the Newsletter Archive that you'll find useful. I'm always adding resources for you on my website and posts on my blog to support your mentoring, so I hope you'll visit from time to time and let me know if I can be of further assistance to you.

So, there's quite a bit to consider as you decide "where to from here" after a mentoring relationship and I hope this book has given you plenty of food for thought!

Subscribe to Mentoring News and receive invitations to free webinars and complimentary ebook.

FREE RESOURCES

N ewsletter, Invitations to **free webinars** and ebook
   Mentoring Demystified here; https://bit.ly/3DH3IJl
   Mentoring Works YouTube Channel, **webinar record-**
ings and short **videos:** https://bit.ly/3dHQe5r
ebooks
How to Lift Team Productivity
https://dl.bookfunnel.com/ji85sra3yc
Many Ways to Mentor
https://dl.bookfunnel.com/4wreeotbej
Mentoring in the Current Crisis
https://dl.bookfunnel.com/jkonfhqdjo
Mentoring Demystified
https://dl.bookfunnel.com/a76ugvevr4
Learning Ladders
https://dl.bookfunnel.com/lugl136sfa
Mentoring – Where to Start
https://dl.bookfunnel.com/4hqrw23ui8
How to Get the Most Out Of Mentoring or Mastermind Groups
https://BookHip.com/PZDJWJN

The Role of the Mentor
https://BookHip.com/SQDNQSV

NOTES

Introduction

1. Randall J Beck and Jim Harter (April 21, 2015) Managers Account for 70% of Variance in Employee Engagement. Gallup Business Journal. https://news.gallup.com/businessjournal/182792/managers-account-variance-employee-engagement.aspx

1. Why Be or Have a Mentor?

1. Noreena Hertz (2010) *How to use experts - and when not to*. Tedsalon, London

4. Mentoring and Learning

1. Wick, Jefferson & Pollock (2008) Getting Your Money's Worth Out of Training and Development. Pfeiffer
2. Center for Creative Leadership. The 70-20-10 Rule for Leadership Development. https://www.ccl.org/articles/leading-effectively-articles/70-20-10-rule/

6. Be Slow to Offer Advice

1. https://www.youtube.com/watch?v=1OADXNGnJok
2. Raggatt, M. (2016) *Lawyers, doctors and public servants in firing line from rise of the machines*. Canberra Times 30 January 2016
   http://www.canberratimes.com.au/act-news/lawyers-doctors-and-public-servants-in-firing-line-from-rise-of-the-machines-20160127-gmf9kt.html
3. Marshal Goldsmith (2007) What Got You Here Won't Get You There
4. M. Bar-Eli, OH Azar, I. Ritov, Y. Keider-Levin, G. Schein (2007) Action bias among elite soccer goalkeepers: The case of penalty kicks. Journal of Economic Psychology
5. Jon M. Jachimowicz, Julia J. Lee, Bradley R. Staats, Jochen I. Menges, Francesca Gino (2016) Commuting as Role Transitions: How Trait Self-Control and Work-related Prospection Offset Negative Effects of Lengthy Commutes. Harvard Business School

7. Discovering Values

1. Berg, A. (1994) *Finding The Work You Love - A Woman's Career Guide.* Resource Publications
2. https://www.knowdellcardsorts.com/Career-Values.cfm

8. On Goals

1. Megginson, D and Clutterbuck, D. (2009) Further Techniques For Coaching and Mentoring
2. https://www.knowdellcardsorts.com/Motivated-Skills.cfm
3. https://store.gallup.com/p/en-au/10385/strengthsfinder-2.0-(hardcover)
4. Statistics Brain (2015) New Years Resolution Statistics http://www.statisticbrain.com/new-years-resolution-statistics/
5. https://www.finder.com.au/top-10-new-years-resolutions
6. Heidi Grant Halvorsen (2012) 9 Things Successful People Do Differently. Harvard Business School Publishing Corporation
7. Carol Dweck (2012) Mindset, How You Can Fulfil Your Potential. Robinson
8. Heidi Grant Halvorson (2011) Why Letting Yourself Makes Mistakes Means Making Fewer of Them. Psychology Today. https://www.psychologytoday.com/au/blog/the-science-success/201102/why-letting-yourself-make-mistakes-means-making-fewer-them
9. Heidi Grant Halvorsen (2012) 9 Things Successful People Do Differently. Harvard Business School Publishing Corporation
10. https://www.youtube.com/watch?v=l9_R5Bvmwjo

9. Mentoring Mindset

1. David Cooperrider, Diana Whitney, Jacqueline Stavros *Appreciative Inquiry Handbook.*
2. Jacqueline Stavros and Gina Hinriches, (2009) *The Thin Book Of SOAR*
3. Marcus Buckingham and Donald Clifton (2001) *Now Discover Your Strengths.* The Free Press.
4. Knowdell's instruments are available from: http://www.careernetwork.org/career_assessment_instr.html
5. Barbara L. Fredrickson, Ph.D. (2009) *Positivity.* Three Rivers Press.
6. Noreena Hertz: *"How to use experts and when not to"* http://www.ted.com/talks/noreena_hertz_how_to_use_experts_and_when_not_to.html
7. John Kenneth Galbraith (1977) *The Age Of Uncertainty.*

10. Strengths-based Development

1. Martin Seligman (1992) *Learned Optimism*. Random House. Australia
2. Martin Seligman (2012) Flourish. Random House. Australia
3. Mihaly Czikszentmihalyi (2008*) Flow*. Harper Collins USA
4. Donald O. Clifton and Marcus Buckingham (2001) *Now Discover Your Strengths*. Simon & Schuster. NY
5. Carol Dweck (2012) *Mindset, How You Can Reach Your Full Potential*. Random House
6. Barbara L. Fredrickson, Ph.D. (2009) *Positivity*. Three Rivers Press.
7. Beth Jones & David Rock *Why the Typical Performance Review Is Overwhelmingly Biased*. Neuro Leadership Institute Blog
   https://neuroleadership.com/your-brain-at-work/quartz-why-the-typical-performance-review-is-overwhelmingly-biased/
8. Brandon Rigoni and Jim Asplund (2016) Global Study: ROI for Strengths-based Development. Gallup Business Journal
9. Glock, J.W (1955) *The relative value of three methods of improving reading*. Ph.D Thesis, University of Nebraska.
10. Donald O. **Clifton** & James K. **Hatter** (2003) *Investing in Strengths*
11. https://www.gallup.com/cliftonstrengths/en/home.aspx

11. Communication Styles for Mentoring

1. Denis Postle,. (1988) *The Mind Gymnasium*. Gaia Books,

12. Build Trust

1. Daniel Siegal The Hand Model of the Brain https://www.youtube.com/watch?v=gm9CIJ74Oxw
2. Addressing 2014 NeuroLeadership Conference, Sydney
3. https://www.brainlinkgroup.com

13. Listen Well

1. Eastwood Atwater (1981) *I Hear You*. Prentice Hall.

14. The Art of Questioning

1. Tasha Eurich (2018) What Self-Awareness Really Is (and How to Cultivate It). Harvard Business Review.
   https://hbr.org/2018/01/what-self-awareness-really-is-and-how-to-cultivate-it

15. Giving and Receiving Feedback

1. Luft, J.; Ingham, H. (1950). "The Johari window, a graphic model of interpersonal awareness". *Proceedings of the western training laboratory in group development* (Los Angeles: UCLA).
2. Dr Matthew White, of Teach For Australia, speaking on *Positive Psychology,* at the Australian Association of Graduate Employers conference, 2010
3. Barbara L. Fredrickson (2013) Updated Thinking on Positivity Ratios. American Psychologist. http://www.thrivere.com.au/assets/frederickson-response-to-flourishing-and-losada-article.pdf
4. Shawn Achor, (2011) The Happiness Advantage. Random House
5. Ken **Blanchard** & Spencer **Johnson** (2009) *The One Minute Manager* Harper-Collins
6. David Rock & Beth Jones (2017) Want to Kill Your Performance Ratings? Here's How to Ensure Success. Strategy and Business blog

Guide to Setting and Getting Goals

1. Heidi Grant Halvorson (2012) *9 Things Successful People do Differently.* Harvard Business Review Press
2. Michael Bungay-Stanier *Building Rock Solid Habits* Part 1,2,3 YouTube https://www.youtube.com/watch?v=l9_R5Bvmwjo

ABOUT THE AUTHOR

Ann Rolfe is a UK-born Australian, living in a small town on the east coast of New South Wales, Australia.

Now retired, Ann Rolfe was a trainer, consultant, and coach. Prior to 2022, she spent over 30 years helping organisations set up and run mentoring programs, train mentors and mentees and provide career development. She is now devoted to making accessible her life's work in mentoring, career and strengths-based development through her books and free webinars.

Her contributions to mentoring were recognised with the 2011 LearnX Asia Pacific Platinum Award for Best Coaching/Mentoring Training Program and in 2013, the New South Wales Juvenile Justice Excellence Award for Innovation.

Internationally respected as a consultant and presenter, her training programs and mentoring materials are used in many countries. Ann has spoken at national and international conferences in Australia, Canada, China, Singapore, The Philippines, and USA. Her regular webinars attract online participants from around the world.

Contact Ann Rolfe
ann@mentoring-works.com

ALSO BY ANN ROLFE

The Mentors Toolkit for Career Conversations

Advanced Mentoring Skills:

Taking Your Conversations to the Next Level